Design for Liberty

1/17/12
To John —
for Everything —

Richard

Design for Liberty

PRIVATE PROPERTY,

PUBLIC ADMINISTRATION,

AND THE RULE OF LAW

Richard A. Epstein

HARVARD UNIVERSITY PRESS

Cambridge, Massachusetts

London, England

2011

Publication of this book has been supported through the generous provisions of the
Maurice and Lula Bradley Smith Memorial Fund.

Library of Congress Cataloging-in-Publication Data

Epstein, Richard A.
Design for liberty : private property, public administration,
and the rule of law / Richard A. Epstein.
p.   cm.
Includes bibliographical references and index.
ISBN 978-0-674-06184-2 (alk. paper)
1. Liberty.   2. Rule of law.   3. Natural law.   4. Right of property—
United States.   5. Rule of law—United States.
6. Law—Political aspects—United States.   I. Title.
K487.L5E65   2011
340'.11—dc22   2011013082

To the third generation—
Bella and Noah Pianko
In hopes for a better world

Contents

Preface

My initial inspiration for writing this book came at a meeting of the John and Jean De Nault Task Force on Property Rights, Freedom, and Prosperity at the Hoover Institution. On multiple occasions thereafter, I presented portions of this book to my Task Force colleagues, from whom I always received intense but constructive criticism. The book's intellectual mission precisely maps the concerns that have animated my work for most of the forty-three years that I have spent in academic work. The matters covered in this book include a set of problems whose importance seems to have grown over time. In working through the details, I would like to thank the indefatigable Lynn Chu for pointing out in a thousand small ways how I might make this manuscript more accessible. I should also like to thank Samantha Bateman, Stanford Law School, class of 2010; Melissa Berger and Jeana Bisnar, New York University Law School, class of 2010; and Isaac Gruber and Sharon Yecies,

University of Chicago Law School, class of 2011, for their patience and precision in reading, correcting, and commenting on the many drafts of this short book. I have presented different parts of this work in many speeches over the years, including at the University of Chicago Law School, at the University of Michigan, and in the Czech Republic and Slovakia. Evidently, the appeal of this issue is well-nigh universal. My thesis is that the current worldwide malaise is reflected in each of the three constituent elements of the title. The protections of private property have eroded. The massive expansion of the public sector has in turn placed heavy demands on public administration, which can be met only by wide-scale disregard of the rule of law. Major changes are needed to reverse the downward trend in civil institutions in the United States and elsewhere. This book contains my diagnosis of the ills, and recipes for the cure.

Design for Liberty

Introduction

From Small to Large Government

Without question, the most profound domestic change in the United States from the beginning of the twentieth century through the present time has been the vast expansion of government under the influence of the progressive worldview that received its highest expression in President Franklin D. Roosevelt's New Deal. Progressive thought was no small perturbation from the views of government that had previously defined the American legal tradition. Indeed, the progressive movement defined itself in opposition to once-dominant classical liberal theories of government that stressed the dominance of private property, individual liberty, and limited government.

The first burst of progressive energy took place during the presidency of Woodrow Wilson, between 1913 and the entry of the United States into World War I in April 1917. Wilson's 1885 book *Congressional Government*[1] was perhaps the most important academic precursor of the progressive political movement. In 1914, nearly thirty years later, Professor Wilson, by then President Wilson, was responsible for creating the Federal Trade Commission, which was meant to add federal heft to individual consumer protection.[2] That same year, Congress passed the Clayton Antitrust Act,[3] which strengthened enforcement of the 1890 Sherman Antitrust Act against businesses, while pointedly exempting both labor unions and agriculture from the antitrust laws.[4] All these statutes increased the number of civil and criminal sanctions that could be brought against ordinary people and firms, for an ever-broader range of offenses.

After the major dislocations of the First World War, there was a temporary abatement of progressive initiatives during the 1920s. However, the 1929 stock market crash quickly ushered in a second wave of reforms that began in the Hoover administration and carried on unabated through Franklin Roosevelt's New Deal, until they were once again cut short by the Second World War. Before then, the notable Hoover landmarks of the early 1930s included the passage of the Smoot-Hawley Tariff,[5] which introduced a worldwide round of protectionist measures; the Davis-Bacon Act of 1931,[6] designed to prevent Southern black laborers from upsetting white union domination in the North; the massive tax increases of the Revenue Act of 1932,[7] meant to close worrisome government deficits; and the Norris-LaGuardia Act of 1932, which limited the power of employers to obtain injunctions in federal court against union activities in labor disputes.[8]

These measures presaged the great structural reforms of Roosevelt's New Deal, including the National Labor Relations Act,[9] which introduced a system of collective bargaining throughout all American industries; the Agricultural Adjustment Acts,[10] which were intended to keep crops priced at cartel levels; the Securities and Exchange Act,[11] intended to rid capital markets of fraud and deception; the Fair Labor Standards Act,[12] which regulated minimum wages and overtime pay, and of course the Social Security system, which sought to introduce a measure of income security for older Americans.[13] Without exception, all of these statutes increased government control over the economy, particularly by strengthening labor and agriculture cartels until they became a fixed feature of the American economy.

The third wave of regulation started under Lyndon Johnson in the 1960s, and continued unabated through the Nixon years in the early 1970s. This round of legislation featured an increased level of transfer payments, both explicit and implicit, from rich to poor through such legislation as the Economic Opportunity Act of 1964.[14] It also included the Civil Rights Act of 1964,[15] and the Medicare[16] and Medicaid[17] statutes of 1965. On other fronts, this third wave of progressive legislation covered environmental protection,[18] endangered species,[19] employee pensions,[20] and workplace safety.[21]

The fourth wave of regulation has thus far lasted through the first two years of the Obama administration, most notably in the Patient Protection and Affordable Care Act ("ObamaCare"), passed in 2010,[22] and the Dodd-Frank Wall Street Reform and Consumer Protection Act of 2010 (the "Dodd-Frank Act").[23] However, the Republican gains in the midterm elections of November 2010 have put a temporary halt to all major initiatives.

For all their substantive differences, each of these legislative initiatives depends heavily on the conscious use of delegated administrative power at both the federal level and the state level. Without exception, these new administrative innovations were designed to displace older legal practices that depended heavily on ordinary civil litigation to vindicate private rights of property and contract. As such, they quickly raised the question of whether or not they were consistent with the rule of law as it applied to the administrative state. No one denied that these rules were laced with all sorts of procedural protections that might apply to individual cases. But with or without protections, these rules conferred on delegated authorities the power to make substantive decisions of far greater scope than had ever been attempted before, and they did so on a massive scale. Not surprisingly, the scope of these new interventions brought forth substantial judicial and intellectual opposition from those who asked how any set of stable property rights could be worth the paper they were printed on if they could be refashioned at any time through some combination of majority will and administrative power. How, too, could any set of individual rights be protected by administrative procedures that operated on a high-volume basis, in disregard of the distinctive position of each individual claimant?

That attack brought forth an equally strong defense by those who followed in the path of Woodrow Wilson, in the belief that administrative actors' high levels of disinterested professional expertise could discipline the passions of a popular majority while simultaneously ridding the American system of the archaic and flawed systems of property and contract that the new economic order, in large measure, displaced. The judicial decisions of the late New Deal, for example, had a near-celebratory air as they demolished one ancient relic after another by the major government initiatives in agricultural and labor markets, Social Security, and securities regulation. When the dust settled, by the onset of World War II, defenders of the older order were dismissed as intellectual troglodytes who were duly exiled to the legal periphery. The situation scarcely changed in the long run, even though the aftermath brought forth some slight retrenchment from New Deal initiatives, most noticeably in the truncation of labor's rights by the Taft-Hartley Act,[24] and more generally by the efforts through the passage of the Administrative Procedure Act of 1946[25] to rein in the discretion of the New Deal agencies.

This short-term reaction did not undo the many reforms of the New Deal. It only placed modest impediments to its operation. The wisdom of these changes is still in doubt, for many self-styled progressives today remain unrepentant insofar as they believe that only a misplaced atavism can justify any lingering affections for the bygone legal order. Indeed, today's more vocal progressive movement increasingly refers back to New Deal prescriptions on government spending as the secret for getting this nation moving again. President Obama has constantly used his favorable view of the New Deal initiatives to justify his efforts to expand the reach of government in such areas as health care, labor law, and environmental protection.[26] The effort here has been to double-down on the original wager that higher levels of government intervention could move an economy out of its past lethargy.

It has not worked. By the end of 2010, the party was over, a victim of its own excesses. Each new layer of regulation has come on top of those that preceded it. Wholly without regard to their particulars, the law of diminishing returns has exerted its powerful hold. The first wave of progressive reform did not topple the economic system, which still left private entrepreneurs free to innovate, and each new wave of regulation has fallen prey to the law of diminishing returns. Newer schemes in each cycle have come at higher costs but promised only reduced benefits. In the final analysis, the level of economic growth has necessarily declined, and by the end of 2010 we had an economy whose many safety nets could not insulate ordinary Americans from a sustained decline in median household incomes and GDP per capita, both of which fell during 2009 and 2010.[27] Month after month, unemployment rates continue stubbornly to hold at just under 10 percent.[28] Although intended to create new jobs in the public sector, a long succession of misguided stimulus programs probably destroyed more jobs than they created in the private sector, through a combination of new taxes and heavy regulation. The recent passage of the health care bill on a bitterly partisan vote has not brought that issue to a close. Rather, the realization that the legislation will usher in an orgy of administrative regulations and criminal sanctions, on topics that go to the heart of how businesses supply and individuals receive health care coverage, has only heightened the unpopularity of the legislation. Business today remains on an investment strike in the face of mounting uncertainties in both capital and labor markets.

In the context of this continued grim news, the intellectual synthesis that seemed so solid at the height of the New Deal is no longer impregnable. At this point, it becomes appropriate to renew the challenges to progressive ideals raised by critics of central planning, such as those posed by Friedrich Hayek in his book *The Road to Serfdom* (1944),[29] and by Milton Friedman in *Capitalism and Freedom* (1962).[30] Both men, and others like them, saw lurking dangers to both political liberty and economic efficiency in the now-dominant social arrangements. It is therefore time for a fresh look not at the particular institutions of our time, but at the intellectual framework that is used to justify our institutional arrangements.

This short book offers one effort to resurrect the twin pillars of an earlier structure. On the substantive side, it urges a return to the classical liberal views on property and contract. On the procedural side, it cautions that the expansion of the administrative state, with its civil and criminal sanctions, is deeply in conflict with traditional values of the rule of law. Over the years in which I've elaborated this agenda, my own views have evolved in ways that turn out to be more sympathetic to government administration than I had once supposed. No amount of devotion to a system of legal rules can eliminate the need for sound discretion in the management of both private and public affairs. Rules may set the framework in which private and public actors make decisions, but when these rules are in place, some degree of discretion must be exercised by those persons in charge of running offices and making the many management decisions that are inherent in taking those executive positions. It is an idle pipe dream to think that even the most ardent devotion to the rule of law can allow government agents and government agencies to dispense with discretion in the day-to-day operation of their business. It is in recognition of that fact that I expanded the title of this book (originally *Private Property and the Rule of Law*) to speak to the vital relationship of public administration to both private property and the rule of law. Over and over again, it has become clear that any system of governance requires government officials to make life-and-death decisions on such questions as who should be charged in a criminal proceeding and who should be hired to perform some critical government job. As a matter of basic management theory, no superior can oversee more than a tiny fraction of the decisions of his or her direct reports, and it is futile to engage in a course of prolonged micromanagement to up that ratio.

The trick is to develop management practices that allow for the needed discretion to be invested in the right individuals, subject to the right level of supervision and control. Therefore, the key point in dealing with the rule of law is to make sure that the tasks that are given to government are both limited and well-defined, and to let the people who are in charge have the degree of flexibility needed to carry out their task. If there is one feature of public administration of law that I attack in this book, it is the peculiar reversal that takes place when courts are willing to "defer" to administrative agencies in the interpretation of the legal language found in statutes and regulations, but feel compelled to flyspeck any government administration decision on where to put a road or to open a school, under the conceit that any decision that does not consider all the right factors, and that ignores all the irrelevant ones, is, in virtue of this fact alone, arbitrary and capricious. No system of extensive judicial oversight of management decisions can displace the need for the sorts of internal checks that good management organizations develop on their own.

In the end, my plea is to marry a set of strong property rights with a system of sound public administration, and much of this book is intended to explain how to satisfy these two imperatives directly. In dealing with these issues, moreover, we must recognize that it is analytically impossible to say that only private-property regimes of classical liberal vintage are logically compatible with the rule of law: all the virtues of neutrality, generality, clarity, consistency, and prospectivity could, in principle, apply to the commands of a well-lubricated administrative state. But, in practice, the thesis of this volume is that this supposed happy equilibrium cannot long sustain itself. Quite simply, the levels of discretion that modern legislation confers on the organs of the administrative state make it impossible to comply with those neutral virtues captured in the rule of law. The point here is not meant as a categorical rejection of all government action, let alone all legislative action; rather, it advocates a sharp recalibration and retrenchment in government's function. The government that can stop the use of dangerous equipment on private construction sites or issue drivers' licenses for the operation of motor vehicles on public roads need not be given the power to plan comprehensively what buildings should be built where and for what purposes people shall take the highways. What it does say is that the more ambitious the government objectives, the more likely it is that the program will result in failure.

To develop this thesis in full, I proceed as follows. Once these philosophical preliminaries are completed in Chapters 1 and 2, I turn to a discussion of the way in which the natural-law and utilitarian traditions approach the question of the rule of law. My point in this discussion is to explain why the insights of the natural-law tradition are essential for outlining the basic conceptions of law, but insufficient to that task. Chapter 3 therefore seeks to explore some of the strengths of that tradition, while Chapter 4 discusses its limitations in forging a comprehensive legal system that melds together both procedural and substantive virtues.

Once these preliminaries are completed, I offer in Chapter 5 a systematic account of the key features of private and common property, in an effort to show how these relatively simple rules work, and how they make it more possible for public institutions to adhere to rule-of-law values, chiefly by controlling the levels of political discretion. Chapter 6 carries this inquiry forward, with a more detailed examination of each of the three major sticks in the bundle of rights—possession, use, and disposition. Chapter 7 then examines how the constitutional limitations on the power of eminent domain dovetail with the understandings of private property under both the classical liberal and progressive conceptions. Chapter 8 extends that analysis to deal with the parallel question of freedom of contract under both systems. Chapter 9 then asks the question of how the various constitutional rules should apply in order to maximize the gain to all parties from those projects that do count as social improvements. Chapter 10 then completes the tour of the substantive issues by examining the responses to questions of income and wealth distribution under these two rival systems.

The last portion of the book examines the difficulties of implementing the rule of law in the modern administrative state. Chapter 11 does so in connection with the rules that deal with key issues of bias and judicial review. Chapter 12 completes the analysis with a discussion of retroactive laws. Chapter 13 follows with an application of these basic principles to explain why key provisions of the Dodd-Frank financial reform and the Obama health care reform necessarily, by their sheer scope, induce compromises that undermine all three elements in the triad of private property, public administration, and the rule of law. A brief conclusion follows, in Chapter 14.

1

The Traditional Conception
of the Rule of Law

The Basic Requirements

The strongest social commitments to both the rule of law and private property long predate the rise of the modern democratic institutions that eventually gave birth to the administrative state. Analytically, the rule of law is, of course, a separate conception from the notions of private property and personal liberty. Nonetheless, there is sometimes a strong impulse on the part of many classical liberal writers to act as if there were some close analytical connection between them. That tie is made explicit when, for example, F. A. Hayek stresses that the requirements of the rule of law are satisfied when the state uses its power to set weights and measures or to prevent the use of force and fraud, but not when it issues to given individuals particularistic commands which are subject to arbitrary powers against other individuals. But even here, Hayek does recognize that a rule-of-law conception must leave some role for state regulation. Accordingly, he makes peace with the administrative state to the extent that he accepts "general and permanent" administrative actions for dealing with "building regulations or factory laws," without paying, it should be added, any close attention to either the content of or the motivation for the passage of those laws.[1] That theme is echoed elsewhere. Writers who deal with such topics as foreign investment constantly remind us that these programs will falter unless a host country gives strong and explicit assurances that contracts will be honored and property will not be expropriated.[2] That worry about the stability of markets often leads to an insistence that the rule of law can be satisfied only under some principle of "nondomination" which easily segues into a decided preference for markets over centralized state planning.[3]

Clearly, the rule of law has a huge role to play in these commercial contexts. But it is important not to overplay a strong hand. The law of common carriers from the earliest times did not operate under competitive principles but required certain key industries—from customs houses to common carriers and network industries in such key sectors as communications, electricity, gas, and power—to supply all customers at reasonable and nondiscriminatory rates under a system of direct public regulation.[4] If the rule of law were exclusively tied to the operation of competitive markets only, these extensive systems, whose operation long predates the modern social democratic state, would also be consigned to some netherworld left unprotected by the rule of law. But in fact it is possible to articulate principles that indicate the ways in which these critical entities ought to be regulated and that are consistent with the rule of law.

Two conclusions follow from these observations. First, any classical liberal system that prizes both liberty and property depends for its operation on a strong commitment to the rule of law. Second, it is clear that the scope of the rule of law cannot be limited to boundaries of the competitive market. As Jeremy Waldron rightly insists, it would be a first-class mistake for classical liberals to insist on some necessary or logical connection between small government systems and the rule of law.[5] A conception of the rule of law has to be broad enough to reach these other areas of human endeavor and thus cannot be too closely tethered to the market. Nor can any conception of the rule of law treat all legal substantive principles as immutable, such that any change in background legal norms necessarily offends its principles. The rise of technology poses questions for the use of the spectrum, the upper airspace, and intellectual property, all of which require some deviation from the traditional notion of property rights. To be sure, continuity has to be valued, but any legal system must, in turn, be responsive to demands for legal change. A conception of the rule of law that is so rigid as to protect the former can easily slight the latter. Finally, and most critically, in principle it is always possible for advanced democracies to respect the procedural requirements of the rule of law without giving strong weight to the protection of either liberty or property, as through the development of extensive procedures that regulate the operation of the expanded administrative state.

In light of these objections, a close connection between the rule of law and classical liberal regimes can be established only empirically by showing, as I hope to do, that the cumulative demands of the modern social democratic state require a range of administrative compromises and shortcuts that will eventually gut the rule of law in practice, even if the state honors it in theory. In order to make that claim, it will become necessary as well to explore the substantive commitments of a strong classical liberal theory in order to show how it accommodates the twin demands of stability and change, which in turn will require a systematic development of the substantive rules that classical liberal theory uses to control state discretion without undercutting the possibility of state order. In order to undertake that task, it is important first to explain the requirements of the rule of law as an abstract principle independent of any substantive commitments.

Historical Evolution

If we are to understand the historical evolution of the rule of law, it is instructive to note that appeals to the rule of law have been part of legal discourse since the earliest times. At its inception, the main function of the rule of law had nothing to do with democratic politics. Rather, its chief function was to negate the arbitrary power of the monarch, which was often encapsulated in a Roman maxim: "Quod principi placuit legis vigorem habet"—"That which is pleasing unto the prince has the force of law." Some translators seek to soft-pedal the starkness of this assertion of royal power by rendering these words in English as "That which seems good to the emperor has also the force of law."[6] This definition seeks to introduce a normative element into the public deliberations of the emperor. But the reality of absolute power, as it exists on the ground, allows for no interposition of reason or discretion between royal command and positive law.[7] The rival conception, that "we live in a nation of laws, not men," represented a concerted effort to constrain what was so often feared: an unbridled exercise of royal power. The oft-maligned theory of natural, or divine, law was instrumental in the struggle to rein in arbitrary royal power. John Locke, in his *Second Treatise of Government,* opens his famous chapter on property rights with a denial that all rights stem from the Crown: "God, as King David says, Psal[m] cxv.16, has given the earth to the children of men; given it to mankind in common."[8]

This explicit appeal to higher authority in support of a bottom-up system of property rights was intended to, and did, exert moral pressure on a monarch who was always immune to any electoral constraints, even if necessarily subject to the political risk of disobedience and rebellion. No modern observer can pretend that these classical rhetorical flourishes, even when they reflected deeply held convictions, worked perfectly. All too often, there were major failures in governance that no set of exhortations, maxims, or institutions could forestall. That said, we should be thankful for small favors. The insistent and fervid repetition of the "natural and divine law" theme surely did no harm, and in some close cases an appeal to the rule of law may have tipped the scales against abuses of state power.

Isolating the elements of the rule of law within this context, however, takes some hard intellectual work. In particular, we must reject the linguistic skepticism of modern philosophical analysis, which places quotation marks around any terms needed to formulate clear rules, which are of course a prerequisite to the rule of law. A philosophical presupposition of the rule of law is that it is possible to articulate and apply legal rules that have some ascertainable content that permits their application to particular settings, not only by lawgivers and judges, but also by ordinary people who have to reflect on the content of desirable legal rules and the proper role of their enforcement. Opponents of classical liberalism, who often take a skeptical approach to the powers of language, despair of offering coherent meanings for terms like "property," "coercion," "nuisance," "causation," "good faith," and "intention of the parties." Thus, in one famous illustration, Robert Lee Hale seeks to destroy the notion of competitive markets by insisting that any refusal to deal counts as a form of coercion that allows for state intervention—a position that effectively guts any notion of voluntary exchange.[9] Similarly, in his highly influential critique of the traditional law of eminent domain, Frank Michelman puts the word "nuisance" in quotation marks on more than twenty separate occasions, so that no one could think that nuisance prevention establishes a strong limitation on the permissible powers of the state to regulate without the payment of just compensation.[10]

Yet on this issue, turnabout is fair play. The same ploy could of course be used against the more ambitious rules of the administrative state—rules pertaining to "discrimination," "disability," "reasonable accommodation," "undue hardship," "equality," "habitat preservation," "social justice," "privilege," "fundamental rights," "adverse environmental impact," and the like. Quite simply, the rule of law requires a degree of linguistic clarity that allows for the articulation of any set of comprehensible rules, regardless of their content, which others can choose to obey or disobey.

To be sure, some of the language of particular rules often falls short of acceptable clarity for context-specific reasons. But this is a far cry from a universal theory of language that is systematically skeptical of the linguistic building blocks of every legal rule, or, worse, selectively skeptical of the clarity of any legal rule that its theorists oppose on substantive grounds. While it is proper to expose ambiguity in particular instances—especially when it can be clarified by better writing—the global view that all language is so unclear as to preclude the formulation of any rules has this dire consequence: it leads to the disintegration of political and legal discourse. This defense of the high level of linguistic coherence does not deny the existence of the hard cases that crop up at the margins under any set of legal rules. Hard cases are endemic to all legal regimes, no matter what their substantive commitments. Pointing these cases out, without further comment, is hardly a decisive argument against any substantive position, be it liberal or conservative, classical or modern.

In practice, the terminological objection can be raised only selectively. After all, no one on the left or the right has a strong incentive to attack the "rule of law" in its most pristine and simplest forms, precisely because the rule of law contains *no* explicit, built-in substantive component. Historically, the rule of law was linked to both natural-law and social-contract theory, both of which were used to explain how to design and implement the escape from the chaos and uncertainty that all individuals face when living in a state of nature. On this point, the Hobbesian model of relentless self-interest is too stark for its own good. Imagine that all human beings act in this way, and no society can escape the corrosive forces that tend to cause its disintegration. Wholly apart from political organizations, however, individuals do not act in a wholly egoist manner. Both the nuclear family and the larger clan are common forms of social organization that predate the state, and they survive because common biological instincts require some level of cooperation, even if only to perpetuate the next generation.

Originally, these clans operated on a moving basis, so that property in chattels and consumables made critical and (permanent) property in land irrelevant, until agriculture drove the need for permanent territories, at which point the formation of states became possible.[11] The complex set of human emotions survived that transformation and thus allowed for some degree of cooperation in the new territorial setting. At some point, the need for an expanded population base meant that the size of the territorial unit had to exceed the size of the clan or tribe, and mechanisms were needed to make sure that outsiders received a level of protection and benefit that let them commit themselves to the group without fear of death or expropriation. At this point, the more distant and formal commands of a system of law had to limit the extent to which personal and familial interests governed the operation of the state. Out of this transition grew the concern with the rule of law as a protective device intended to earn the allegiance of all subjects or citizens of the state.

These broad historical strokes cannot conceal that most efforts to form political states failed. Transitions are always difficult. Even today, many small family businesses founder in their efforts to grow. So, too, many primitive societies came apart at the seams because of their well-known inability to prevent the faction, strife, and discord that can sink many a collective endeavor. But in those societies that did survive, the Lockean instincts have proved largely sound in basic outline, even if wanting on matters of detail. Most people do have a strong sense of self-interest, albeit one tempered by an awareness of the rights of others. There are strong built-in imperatives about harm and reciprocity that most people respect most of the time. Natural inclination, socialization, and informal social norms help to keep people in line. But "most" people decidedly does not mean "all" people. Many law-abiding citizens (as we used to say) share the strong perception that a small number of dangerous individuals could destabilize a fragile peace, to the ruination of all other people who are prepared to play by the rules of the game.

So why then take the risk of forming governments whose monopoly over the use of force can also lead to abuse? Only because the alternatives are worse. As Locke insisted, in the state of nature, "[t]here wants an *established,* settled and known *law,* received and allowed by . . . common measure to decide all controversies between [men]."[12] The needed rules are meant to be (as they are often not today) "plain and intelligible."[13] State power also remedies the want of a "*known and indifferent Judge,* with authority to determine all differences according to the established law."[14] The same concern with discretion is evident in the American Founding period, where both Federalists and Antifederalists shared a common fear of excessive discretion in the executive and judicial branches.[15]

The modern formulations tend to track these concerns as well. In speaking about the evolution of the rule of law, A. V. Dicey stressed the criminal side of the equation when he wrote:

> When we say that the supremacy or the rule of law is a characteristic of the English constitution, we . . . mean, in the first place, that no man is punishable or can be lawfully made to suffer in body or goods except for a distinct breach of law established in the ordinary legal manner before the ordinary Courts of the land. In this sense the rule of law is contrasted with every system of government based on the exercise by persons in authority of wide, arbitrary, or discretionary powers of constraint.[16]

Hayek harps on the same theme when he writes of the rule of law: "Stripped of all technicalities, [the rule of law] means that government in all its actions is bound by rules fixed and announced beforehand—rules which make it possible to foresee with a fair degree of certainty how the authority will use its coercive powers in given circumstances, and to plan one's individual affairs on the basis of this knowledge." All of this is done not with the expectation of perfection, but so that "the discretion left to the executive organs wielding coercive power should be reduced as much as possible."[17] Although Hayek does not in so many words mention the judicial system, it clearly must limit executive power in order for the overall system to have a fair measure of success. These requirements do not all deal with substance, but they do try to force decisionmaking into paths which will indirectly rule out inferior social outcomes. Put otherwise, the rule of law virtues can be regarded as instrumental tools that are suitable to the achievement of sound ends, so much so that they become almost ends in themselves. In light of their ubiquitous role and critical functionality, it is worth looking at them in some greater detail, starting with the judiciary, and then working backward to the other branches of government.

The Rule against Bias

When Locke articulated his normative framework, he was not writing on a blank slate by thinking about the central role that courts play in any legal system dedicated to the rule of law. The most famous articulation of the rule against bias at the common law is found in *Dr. Bonham's Case,* decided by Sir Edward Coke in 1610.[18] The narrow point in that decision was that the Royal College of Physicians could not imprison or fine Thomas Bonham for practicing medicine without a license when the board had a financial interest in the outcome of the case. The point here is that the *appearance* that justice has been done is critical, for there is no reason at all for the same party to both perform the act and benefit from it, so long as it is possible to separate the two functions, which can easily be accomplished by trying the case before an independent party. The one exception to this position, moreover, relates to the doctrine of "necessity"—a theme that recurs throughout the classical liberal system—which permits some judge to hear cases when all judges are subject to some form of bias, so long as the judge takes exceptional care to guard against actual bias. No one should go free from legal sanction because the magnitude of his wrong makes it impossible for any neutral judge to be in a position to hear his case.

Coke treated the control of bias as so central to the rule of law that he used *Dr. Bonham's Case* as the springboard for the larger proposition that principles of natural justice could trump the English principle of parliamentary sovereignty. "The common law will control acts of parliament, and sometimes adjudge them to be utterly void: for when an act of parliament is against common right and reason, or repugnant, or impossible to be performed, the common law will control it, and adjudge such act to be void."[19] William Blackstone rejected the broader principle in his defense of parliamentary supremacy,[20] but it has worked its way into American law as one of the key components of the due process of law protected by both the Fifth and Fourteenth Amendments.

Beyond Bias

The issue of bias is but one part of a larger concern with the rule of law that has also been articulated in modern times. In this connection, it is useful to set out the procedural requirements that Lon Fuller defended with such elegance when he articulated his own natural-law theory in *The Morality of Law*.[21] Although Fuller does not speak of these as components of the rule of law, they are widely regarded as such.[22]

Eight Routes of Failure for any Legal System

1. The lack of rules or law, which leads to ad hoc and inconsistent adjudication.
2. Failure to publicize or make known the rules of law.
3. Unclear or obscure legislation that is impossible to understand.
4. Retroactive legislation.
5. Contradictions in the law.
6. Demands that are beyond the power of the subjects and the ruled.

7. Unstable legislation (ex. daily revisions of laws).
8. Divergence between adjudication/administration and legislation.

Equality: In Principle and in Practice

A quick inspection indicates that none of Fuller's core concerns implicates any substantive position. Rather, the common thread that links these concerns together is that they amplify the Lockean concern for established, settled, and known law of general application. Each element of Fuller's picture is aimed at providing individuals with a predictable set of laws under which they can govern their conduct to avoid civil or criminal sanctions. It is easy to disparage Fuller's mundane rules for their trivial intellectual content or practical unimportance in the grand scheme of things. Such a smug attitude is possible, however, only when these conditions are routinely satisfied so that they are taken for granted. But the social situation quickly turns dire when they are systematically flouted. It matters little that we can find some overlap and duplication in the articulation of these rules. Such inelegance or redundancy does not detract from their basic function of offering some minimalist embodiment of the word "rule" as it appears in the phrase "rule of law." At their core, these principles offer safeguards against the ad hoc application of state power against individuals or groups singled out for special treatment by either the criminal-justice or the civil-justice system.

On these matters, articulating the formal principles of the rule of law offers a useful start but not a complete answer in line with Fuller's basic principles. The late Judge Henry Friendly listed some of the key components as follows: the right to appear before an unbiased panel; the right to have notice of charges and the reasons for them; the right to an opportunity to present argument and evidence, including the right to present witnesses; the right to hear and cross-examine opposing witnesses; the right to have the decision based solely on the record; the right to have counsel; and the right to obtain a reasoned opinion, based on written findings that are subject to review.[23] In one sentence: Those formal rules should provide each person with notice of the charges and the opportunity to present his or her case before the neutral public official designated to decide the case. Ex parte, or one-sided, procedures may be needed to run investigations to see whether private parties ought to be charged. Sometimes they are also needed in order to initiate some public action, such as a preliminary injunction against acts that pose a serious risk of imminent harm to life or limb. But these unilateral procedures are never appropriate in order to conclusively resolve any dispute that removes or infringes the rights and liberties of others. The right to be heard on matters of both law and fact is yet another condition of a free and prosperous society.

Fuller also echoes Locke and Hayek in his insistence that laws be published in advance and in clear form for all to see. Here again, the sovereign maintains complete control over the content of the rules, which could themselves be harsh, unwise, or counterproductive. But public and known laws should always displace secret and variable rules, which open up opportunities for political intrigue. Further, Fuller's concern with unclear laws naturally follows from his preceding concern with unpublished ones. What good is publication if it generates incomprehension? The fact that learned intermediaries can help to soften the risk of incomprehensible laws affords little comfort to individuals who are held responsible for disregarding laws that they do not understand. Similarly, Fuller's general prohibition against *retroactive* laws ensures that people are judged by the rules in place when they act, not by rules brought to bear later on, when the popular mood may have shifted radically. Next, the fear of contradiction represents an effort to avoid putting people into impossible positions where they are simultaneously required to perform and to refrain from performing the same act on pain of criminal punishment or civil liability. Unstable laws raise similar concerns, if people have to recalibrate their conduct on a daily basis to meet any changes in the law. Finally, the issue of divergence between adjudication and administration on the one hand, and legislation on the other, goes to the core of any uneasiness about the expansion of the administrative state. Agents charged with the enforcement of law should not have a blanket license to remake the law in their own image.

It is critical to note that Fuller's minimum conditions for a sound social order are placed under constant pressure in all legal systems, in ways that Fuller, writing before the explosion of modern law, could not have imagined. The need to keep true to rule-of-law values arises in all civil proceedings, where individual plaintiffs normally can make an unbridled election on whether or not to sue. That litigation, of course, involves the threat of the use of public force against a recalcitrant defendant. Yet by the same token, when the plaintiff has a valid claim, the refusal to pay operates as a form of coercion in the opposite direction. Here is no place to offer an extensive disquisition on how the rules of pleading and proof should operate across the board, from simple accident to huge antitrust cases, where the choice of the correct rules on pleading, discovery, and appeal could make or break a system. Instead, the more limited function is to note that errors in the formulation of civil-procedure rules increase in importance as the stakes get higher.

A second problem that dogs all legal systems is that of deciding how to classify which persons or groups should be singled out for special treatment. On this, an appeal to the rule of law gives at most uncertain guidance. The correct rule is not that all cases should be treated alike, but rather that like cases should be treated alike. So which cases are alike? This task is easily side-stepped when all persons are subject to the same legal requirements, as with general prohibitions against murder or theft. But in many situations, that level of generality is inappropriate. The rules dealing with driving do not apply to nondrivers. The rules that regulate new construction need not take the same form as the rules that regulate the rehabilitation of older structures, given the different types of risk. In many contexts, applying rules too broadly can be dangerous. So we must save the basic intuition here by noting that the rules in question apply to individuals that operate in particular roles. Therefore, so long as any individual of full age and capacity can aspire to fulfill those roles, the generality requirement seems satisfied for state regulation. There can be no abuse by allowing only drivers the privilege of using the public highway, and so on down the line. But even this response is not perfect, because it could well be perfectly rational to impose stricter requirements on chauffeurs and taxi drivers than on ordinary drivers.

At this point, the appeal to formal principles alone buckles under the strain. Necessarily, therefore, it seems that some substantive consideration is needed to give content to the rule of law. Individuals in direct competition with each other should be subject to the same constraints, placing a heavy burden of proof on those who wish to discriminate within given categories. Put otherwise, if the classifications tend to promote public safety, they make sense. To the extent that they tend to skew opportunities from one group to another, they do not. One illustration of the principle comes from trade across national or state lines. In these instances, the correct nondiscrimination rule allows the state to impose the same restrictions on outsiders that it imposes on its own members, which leaves both groups subject to regulation intended to deal with, for example, health and safety risks. Yet even when this nondiscrimination rule is accepted in theory, it can easily be derailed in practice by imposing, for example, a more stringent inspection regime for goods coming from out of state than for those that are made or sold within it. It is one of the signal achievements of the American system that the set of legal rules developed to combat this form of disguised protectionism at state boundary lines has been so successful.[24]

Prosecutorial Discretion under the Rule of Law

The same challenges to Fuller's principles also arise in determining the proper scope and use of prosecutorial discretion in criminal cases. Fuller's principles are not potent enough to deny prosecutors the right to examine the facts of individual cases to see whether some enforcement action is justified, and if so, which. On this topic, it is alluring, but unwise, to assert, as did the late Herbert Wechsler, that the exercise of prosecutorial discretion cannot operate so long as prosecutors may act "without reference to any norms but those that they may create for themselves."[25] This position surely is correct if it means that independent prosecutors within a given office can each go off in his or her own direction, without internal supervision. But in most cases, the most powerful form of supervision is likely to come from within the office, as sound management principles force individual prosecutors to account to their superiors, fellows, and (yes) subordinates under standard protocols whose use is backed up by the careful collection and use of statistical data from both within and outside the office. On this point, I think that there is much to commend in the thesis propounded by professors Marc Miller and Ronald Wright: "We believe that the internal office policies and practices of thoughtful chief prosecutors can produce the predictable and consistent choices, respectful of statutory and doctrinal constraints, that lawyers expect from traditional legal regulation."[26] Done right, as they report from their own studies in New Orleans, Milwaukee, Charlotte, and San Diego, this approach works.

The basic insight boils down to one critical proposition. The rule of law must distinguish between government officials as regulators and government officials as managers. In the former role, the key is to develop, whenever possible, bright-line rules to govern primary behavior, which limits government discretion.[27] In government's management role, however, the most that can be asked of any government official is to exercise sound discretion in the same way that is demanded in any private business where officers and directors have fiduciary responsibilities. Both in government and in business, the job at the center is to make sure that there is a consistent and uniform execution of basic policy at the periphery. Ordinary business customers bridle at inconsistent treatment of similar claims. The need for that uniformity in treatment is even greater when prison sentences or heavy fines are the outgrowth of decision.

Accordingly, it is only careful management that can control the multiple variables needed to run any public prosecutor's office. The many good reasons not to prosecute are usefully catalogued by Miller and Wright: the accused is being prosecuted for some other charge; the victim refuses to cooperate with the prosecution; the testimonial or physical evidence is insufficient to support the charge; substantive or procedural defenses have a strong likelihood of success; witnesses cannot be located or persuaded to speak.[28] Juggling these and other variables is not a job for rules-based judicial oversight, which is far too intermittent and removed to have any real chance of success. That work is properly the business of public officials, who have to be acculturated to their proper role. Never underestimate the ability of unguided judicial intervention to roil well-run public businesses by upsetting sound decisions by seasoned professionals.

Within this framework, judicial oversight still has one key role, which is to secure compliance with key minimum norms against egregious behaviors that can be externally enforced. Prosecutors undertake their investigation by reference to substantive and procedural norms of general applicability. Forced confessions and perjured testimony can be sharply punished. Racial and ethnic prejudice can be resisted. In these cases, the same *nondiscrimination* principle that works in dealing with many interstate or international trade disputes can well help, albeit in a more limited fashion, to prevent public officials from singling out their enemies for retribution under rules that they would never apply to their friends. These *selective* prosecutions may be narrower in scope than general ones, but prosecutors' higher level of discretion does open some windows that let state power be used for exacting retribution.

This ever-present risk of selective prosecution reveals the danger in the common maxim that "the greater power implies the lesser power." This maxim is often invoked to suggest that the prosecutor who is entitled to bring cases against all should be allowed, willy-nilly, to bring them against any subset of potential defendants at his or her own choosing. But it is a mistake to assume that because it is all right to go after all, it is all right to go after only some. This supposed syllogism misses the basic point that the power to select some and exclude others is, in political terms, a "greater" power than the power to prosecute all under some neutral standard. It is much harder to go after one's political enemies if it is necessary also to go after one's friends.

In modern American law, the elusive doctrine of "unconstitutional conditions" represents an explicit repudiation of this "greater/lesser" theory by imposing extensive limitations on any principle of selection that, in line with our earlier discussion, is systematically designed to advance one group at the expense of another. The government may be entitled to either give or withhold benefits from any individual, but it is not therefore entitled to condition the transfer of benefits upon a waiver of constitutional rights.[29] Thus, it may be possible to exclude all drivers between ages eighteen and twenty-one from the public roads. But it is not permissible to grant licenses to Democrats over age twenty-one while denying those licenses to Republicans of the same age. At this point, the analysis necessarily makes references to the substantive consequences of the particular legislation, which again vividly shows the fragility of any formal conception of the rule of law that is consciously devoid of any substantive commitments.

Here are two vivid recent examples. Everyone senses the uneasiness in a rule that allows someone to go free from criminal prosecution in exchange for supporting changes in the criminal law that the prosecutor champions before the legislature. Yet just this sort of condition was imposed in settlements of criminal charges against insurance brokers in New York State for taking "contingent commissions," whereby the brokers' net earnings depended in part on the loss history of their insureds. Brokers who recommended customers with good loss records received a rebate from the insurer. The brokerage firm was required, at the very least, not to speak publicly against changes in the rules governing the use of these commissions desired by the then attorney general, Eliot Spitzer.[30]

Here is another example. It is surely appropriate to settle class action lawsuits with payments to class members. But it is quite a different thing to insist that part of the payments be made to the law school from which the prosecutor graduated, to support its ethics program. Yet just that happened when Christopher Christie, now the governor of New Jersey but then the U.S. attorney for the District of New Jersey, entered into a deferred prosecution of Bristol-Myers-Squibb for a violation of the securities law, so long as the company made a contribution to the ethics program at Seton Hall Law School, from which Christie had graduated.[31] What turns out to be a fortuitous gift in the one case could lead to efforts by private parties to seek this kind of bounty by turning suitable targets over to the prosecutors. Working through the implications of these simple examples requires a coherent theory of what counts as a constitutional right. It is best to postpone the application of this crucial principle until after we discuss the substantive elements embedded in the rule of law within the framework of classical liberal theory.

Legislative Matters

The classical liberal system is concerned not only with setting out the appropriate rules of conduct for judicial proceedings, but also with delineating the structure of legislative institutions. Defenders of the rule of law, in recognizing the need to discipline the use of coercive power, commonly support political structures with built-in divisions of legal power in order to slow down the legislative decisionmaking process. It is no accident that the drafters of the American Constitution, under the evident influence of Montesquieu's *Spirit of the Laws,*[32] adopted a complex system with two such divisions built in on the ground floor: a separation-of-powers principle that allocated power among the three branches of the federal government, and a federalist system that divided authority between the single national and the many state governments—which could clash with one other as easily as they could with the federal government. The key driver for these institutional arrangements was the drafters' desire to combat the recurrent danger of factionalism.[33] Both of these structural features contain instructive ambiguities.

On the first division, the United States Constitution separates federal powers by vesting legislative power in Congress (Article I), executive power in the President (Article II), and judicial power in the Supreme Court (Article III). For these purposes, the precise location of these lines and the enormous complexity that they generate are far less important than the underlying philosophical motivation for their adoption. The drafters divided power among the branches in order to erect a content-free barrier against passing new legislation, driven by the fear that any new law would likely do more harm than good, given the diverse and selfish motives of political actors. Furthermore, this regime created a strong presumption against delegating large policy decisions to administrative bureaucrats in subordinate positions who operate outside the glare of public restraint. Once again, the impulse is not new, for it follows the old Roman maxim, "Delegatus non potest delegare": "The delegatee may not delegate." As with the rule of law, these two presumptions are free of any express or implicit substantive commitments.

In these broad classifications, one recurring theme concerns the lack of perfectly demarcated boundaries between the permissible activities of the various branches. And while there is no one test that covers all of the hard marginal cases, one principle helps to organize discordant results. For example, Congress has the power to build post offices and to establish post roads. But must it quite literally specify the exact location in each town on which the President or his Postmaster General—one of the first four cabinet positions, along with state, treasury, and (as it was then known) war—can build? The answer is surely no, for there must be some play in the joints. Similarly, corporations and charitable institutions often divide power between their boards of directors and their chief executive officer. Yet no one thinks that this division is either useless on the one hand or perfectly precise on the other. Rather, an appeal to the twin notions of separation of power and its working partner, checks and balances, helps to organize the distribution of government powers. It does not decide authoritatively, however, whether Congress can use its power to regulate war to order the President as Commander-in-Chief to open a second front in an ongoing war. But no matter how intractable the questions of delegation, the one constant limitation on executive power is simply this: where there is no legislation, there can be no execution, for there is no class of "inherent powers" to undertake fresh initiatives large or small, either in the American Constitution or in the accounts of executive power found in Locke and Montesquieu. Locke hit the nail on the head when he wrote: "But because the laws, that are at once, and in a short time made, have a constant and lasting force, and need a perpetual execution, or an attendance thereunto; therefore it is necessary there should be a power always in being, which should see to the execution of the laws that are made, and remain in force. And thus the legislative and executive power come often to be separated."[34] It is always possible to quibble about these differences at the margin, but the existence of these marginal cases should not preclude application of general principles in the many clear cases.

At this point, the critical issue becomes substantive. The distribution of easy and hard cases is not a fixed fact of nature. Much depends on the articulation of the relevant constitutional scheme. A government could issue drivers' licenses to individuals who have passed a standardized test, or it could issue permits to practice medicine to those who have taken a course of study leading to a standardized professional examination, or it could issue a permit to build skyscrapers to builders whose blueprints have been extensively reviewed for safety. The modern administrative state, of course, does not confine its operation to these modest tasks, but expands its scope by orders of magnitude beyond the traditional notions of health and safety. This newer expansion of police power, in turn, places greater pressure on both the rule of law and private-property rights in such matters as licensing new dams, hospitals, schools, and power plants, often for reasons that have nothing to do with either health or safety, but that reflect a variety of disputable aesthetic or dangerous anticompetitive motives.

At this point, the sheer matter of scale in governance puts insistent stress on both the rule of law and the protection and use of private property. Before turning to those concerns, however, we must discuss how the traditional conceptions of economic liberty and private property dovetail with respect to the rule of law. Doing this requires rethinking the system from the ground up. Accordingly, it is useful to connect classical liberal thought back to its historical origins in both the natural-law and utilitarian traditions, which overlap on many questions, but which take different paths on others. It is more instructive to start with the overlap between these two traditions. Thereafter, we can identify the limitations in natural-law theory that point to adopting an explicit utilitarian approach that evaluates all laws in light of their systematic consequences for society as a whole.

2

Reasonableness Standards
and the Rule of Law

The previous chapter drew a sharp distinction between the discretion that public officials need to exercise in discharging their legal responsibilities and the hard edges of property rights. In that analysis, the entire effort was to banish the elements of reasonableness and good faith from the overall equation. As a general matter, this approach surely has to be too aggressive, for virtually every legal system must, at some point or another, incorporate these elements into its substantive rules. It would be unwise to assume that the mere mention of these open-ended terms necessarily renders a legal system noncompliant with the rule of law. Yet by the same token, it would be equally unwise to assume that each and every mention of these pliable terms is necessarily consistent with the rule of law. The challenge in this chapter is to figure out how to separate the proper and improper appeals to these concepts.

At first blush, it seems tempting to say that all effort to produce a legal system that advances social welfare could simply ignore matters of reasonableness and fair play. On this view, the truncated inquiries demanded by strict corrective-justice principles look to be antithetical to any utilitarian conception of justice. As a general matter, however, the exact opposite is true. The object of a utilitarian theory is to reach sound results. It is not to make all the pluses and minuses of the litigants the source of their rights and duties in practical contexts where the costs of dispute resolution must necessarily be factored into the equation. Like personal happiness, social welfare is best achieved by indirection. Make happiness the purpose of every action, and it is easy to be miserable. One should do particular tasks that one enjoys, and happiness flows from the harmonious succession of philosophically unreflective acts. Enforce ordinary contracts, and both parties to the contracts are better off. Increase the wealth of trading partners, and the opportunities for gains to third parties increase as well. Repeat the same simple exercise of voluntary exchange and cooperation countless times, and achieving social welfare is a task that will take care of itself. Why? Because the regime of freedom of contract works well for most small-numbered transactions that rest on a stable distribution of property rights.

At this point, it is prudent to hoist a warning flag. Utilitarian concerns play a critical role in designing the rules of the road for human interaction. But the system often runs best when the functional reasons for those rules are kept in the background in the course of resolving individual disputes. To keep with the highway example, the decision on how to install stoplights should be made with an eye toward getting the most value out of the highway system at the lowest cost. There can, on this view, be genuine disputes as to whether there is enough traffic at a given intersection to warrant the installation of a traffic light. But once that determination is made by a transportation authority, it is a huge mistake to require its revalidation under some generalized reasonableness standard after every individual intersection collision. Institutional considerations block the high degree of individualization of disputes so prized by moralists.

Accordingly, the correct approach treats the underlying soundness of the rules as a given in the course of litigation, and then resolves any dispute simply by asking which party or parties deviated from the rules of the road. There are enormous benefits in using concrete rules as the way station between a grand theory of social utility and the resolution of individual disputes. Indeed, one of the great mistakes in modern tort law has been to promote cost-benefit analysis by adopting a global legal regime that purports to hold negligent any person who "does not exercise reasonable care under all the circumstances," which in turn include "the foreseeable likelihood that the person's conduct will result in harm, the foreseeable severity of any harm that may ensue, and the burden of precautions to eliminate or reduce the risk of harm."[1] Judicial decisions should not elevate a cost-benefit analysis from its useful rule as background heuristic to the sole decisionmaking tool in individual cases, where the test misleads far more often than it informs.[2]

The point becomes clear when we contrast the use of this negligence system in highway accidents with the use of the same supposed standard in cases brought against product manufacturers for design defects. With the highway cases, the level of judicial discretion is constrained by the rules of the road, which set out in advance a known framework with which all must comply. Within that highly articulated environment, the function of the law of negligence is solely to allow for excuses in a few cases in which individuals are so overborne, for example, by epilepsy or a stroke, that they cannot comply with any rule at all, even one designed for their own self-protection. Even in these cases, the usual legal formulation rejects that narrow class of excuse where the individual had some earlier premonition of the future potential breakdown.

In these cases, the better rule is to ignore both the epileptic condition and the earlier warnings and to apply the uniform rule that looks solely to the deviation from the rules of the road. In yet another application of the proposition that simple rules work best in a complex world, removing both of these individuated elements from the case increases the reliability of decisionmaking while reducing administrative costs—both benefits that are shared by all parties within the system. This rule-based system, with limited exceptions, is far more likely to comport with the rule of law than a set of loose standards that inevitably give ample play to judicial discretion in their routine application. Fortunately, the day-to-day resolution of disputes tends to follow just these guidelines, except in the large cases that go up on appeal.[3]

The argument here is not that a reasonableness or good-faith standard is unintelligible. It is that they do not lend themselves to a quick and easy resolution of the vast majority of individual cases. On the conceptual point, it is, however, too easy to plump for one rule on the ground that the rival conception makes no sense.

Here is one example taken from tort law. Quite often, activities on the land of one person can cause destruction, as by fire, on the land of another. One recurrent question is whether the duty that the keeper of a fire owes to his neighbors should be framed in terms of "good faith" or "reasonable care under the circumstances," where the latter is understood to be more exacting than the former. In one key case on the subject, *Vaughan v. Menlove*,[4] each of these standards was attacked on the ground of its incurable vagueness. Both of these attacks have to be wrong: each of these wavy standards has its place in the law, for each is subject to a reasonably rigorous interpretation. "Good faith," in this context at least, means that an actor should in principle weigh the interest of another as equal with his own in making decisions under conditions of uncertainty, but absolves the decisionmaker of the consequences of innocent error. "Reasonable care," for its part, refers to the condition where a party is asked to take precautions up to the point where their expected costs at the margin equal their expected benefits.

The meanings of both standards are clear enough.[5] Ironically, however, neither of these standards should govern in connection with harm caused to third parties, where a strict liability standard (in which all forms of negligence or bad faith are irrelevant) better protects innocent parties from harm inflicted by the defendant. To be sure, the application of these standards is often fraught with difficulty in close cases. But so what? Marginal disputes are an inevitable part of all legal systems, which is why no set of legal rules is self-enforcing. The key question is not whether there are close cases in which it is easy to come out the other way.

Rather, the ideal solution is one that seeks to use hard-edged rules in the majority of cases, reserving the softer conceptions of reasonableness and good faith for a limited subset of cases. It is the failure to get this demarcation correct which has led to so much difficulty in modern areas of tort law, such as those dealing with medical errors or defective products. The secret here lies in the insight that the proper role of the reasonableness and good faith standards is *exclusively* to back up the basic reliance on the rules of the road. However well the strict traffic rules (for example) work in most cases, they cannot cover the entire range of permutations. In some cases, that approach falls short because exclusive reliance on the rules of the road ignores the *interactions* that do and should take place when one party becomes aware that the other has deviated from the rules. In these cases, it is no longer acceptable for the party who is alerted to the dangers created by others to act as if he did not have that information. He cannot just continue to drive forward when someone is seen to block his way, solely because he has the right of way.

The question then arises: Precisely what sort of *reaction* is required of parties who are alert to the risks of their actions to the bodily integrity and private property of others? Sticking doggedly to the older rules of the road in the face of new information can lead to mayhem, and is the one option that is entirely off the table. No driver may deliberately run down a pedestrian who is crossing against the light, solely because he has the right of way. The decisive question is what forms of evasive action are incumbent upon him. The short answer is that the nature and types of needed and appropriate deviation from accepted rules of the road cover such a wide variation that it is impossible to specify them in advance with rule-like precision in an individual case. Peril comes from all sources in all sorts of unanticipated ways. Generally speaking, all that can be known is that there will be inevitable tradeoffs between slowing down and swerving, for example, that cannot be identified in advance.

Faced with this menu of unappetizing choices, the proper global response is to ask only that an individual do the best that he or she can under the circumstances. Placing the issue in this light invites an examination of both the capabilities of the actor in emergency situations and the pluses and minuses of the choices shown, without the benefit of hindsight. Once the egg is broken, there is no way to put it back together again. Yet we must remember that these countless variations on the so-called legal doctrine of "last clear chance" take place only in the few cases where the rules have broken down.[6] They do not dispense with the rules altogether. But so long as no one can think of a set of rules that works equally well in all cases, "reasonableness under the circumstances," in light of the imperfect capabilities of the actor, is the best standard that is humanly obtainable, and cannot therefore be thought to clash with the requirements of the rule of law. The key point is that the low frequency of these occurrences does not undermine the workability of the basic rules of the road in the huge majority of cases. Yet by the same token, if one were to excuse all teenage drivers on the basis of their youth, the rate of dislocations would be far more pronounced, which is why modern rules of highway liability reject this position.[7] In mass interactions with anonymous individuals, no one can be expected to make allowances for the misconduct of others. Teenagers should learn to drive in parking lots.

The question then arises whether negligence tests that are good in some circumstances can be prudently generalized into some grand over-arching principle of liability. They cannot. The negligence test does not operate well in cases of product design and warning defects when it is systemically unmoored from the constraints of the highway rules. Left unbounded, that test decides every situation as if it were an emergency case by asking in a thousand different guises whether one design could be challenged on the ground that it is inferior to some alternative design that, all things considered, is safer under the circumstances, without, of course, being so prohibitive in cost that the whole system breaks down. At this point, the level of discretion conferred on juries, or for that matter on judges, to redesign products after the accident has occurred, collides with the standard concerns of the rule of law. It is impossible to know which of an infinite number of alternative designs is feasible, when none have been tried. With the benefit of hindsight, it is easy to think solely in terms of design changes that prevent the accident that did occur, while ignoring the other vulnerabilities that the new design creates. The ad hoc nature of what James Henderson called "polycentric judgments" offers good testimony that the use of a single term— "negligence"—can cover a multitude of different legal decision rules that have little or nothing in common with one another.[8] It is, therefore, important to recognize that even instances of common-law decisionmaking can fall prey to the same weaknesses as administrative determinations if they adopt open-ended standards that make it impossible for any impartial observer to decide whether a decision is right or wrong.

A closer look at the comparison between highway accidents and more adventurous and modern types of medical malpractice and product liability cases clinches the point. This new breed of malpractice and product cases often offers the soothing assurance that the new standards of liability are just another manifestation of the older standard of "reasonable care taken under all the circumstances."[9] In medical malpractice cases, thousands of individual decisions are made, some of which are surely wrong under a simple test that asks whether the physician or other health care professional acted reasonably under the circumstances. Product designs and warnings can be configured in thousands of different ways, some of which are sure to be found deficient if the only standard is whether they are reasonable under the circumstances.

In order to prevent just that potential explosion of unfettered jury discretion, the traditional tort law—that is, the tort law that governed before the major expansion in liability that took place between around 1960 and 1980—in both of these areas developed powerful stops that restrained the use of these free-form formulas. The inflexible standard of care in medical settings was that of "customary practice," derived from inside the medical profession, and not imposed from without.[10] While it did not, and could not, provide guidelines with the precision of a median strip in a public road, it did go a long way toward limiting the levels of discretion found in these cases.

Similarly, with the potential scope of product liability, the traditional keystone asked whether the defendant had created some concealed defect that caused harm when used in the ordinary fashion.[11] In some cases, the trap could be removed by redesigning the product. But in others, with many drugs and chemicals, the risk was an inseparable side effect of a useful product. At that point, the appropriate response was to warn about the condition in question, so that the downstream user, be it a physician or professional on one hand, or a consumer or employee on the other, could make intelligent choices about product uses. The system worked well because in both design and warning settings, it led to the orderly transmission of information to downstream product users who were then in a position to accept or decline the risk in question. In effect, the system pushed both upstream and downstream parties to act in the optimal cooperative fashion with respect to those products that made it through the standard distribution channels. The downstream users had a right to expect that the product in question conformed to these basic standards.

Note the desirable incentive effects of this regime. Products with truly dangerous configurations could not get sold once the necessary disclosures were made—a limitation that created a constant pressure toward product improvement. But once that was done, the upstream supplier had the right to assume that the downstream user would make the normal and proper use of the product. The legal rules thus pushed both parties into an equilibrium position, with high levels of performance at all points in the chain of distribution. With respect to all parties, the effort was to avoid the open-ended reasonableness inquiry which asks them to figure out what to do in light of the anticipated misconduct of others. Joint levels of compliance lead to fewer accidents, and thus the strength of the system lies not only in its ability to reduce the cost of those accidents that do occur, but in its greater ability to reduce the level of accidents in the first instance. Within the traditional organization of the field, questions of unreasonableness arose only in those few cases where, for example, an automobile driver was confronted by a sudden mechanical failure. With quality and design improvements, product liability becomes a backwater of the law.

The rejection of this model has led to the opposite result: a thousand-fold expansion of liability over an earlier generation. Yet there is no evidence that this expansion in tort liability has done anything to improve product safety.[12] This lack of improvement is exactly what we should expect from the conscious decision of modern judges to detach the use of reasonableness tests from their specific institutional context, so that they take over all adjudication in all major litigated cases. No longer does the issue of reasonableness arise after it has been established that the defendant hit the plaintiff. The requirement of the direct use of force thus narrows the inquiry to the point where the reasonableness inquiry deals only with a narrow set of excuses, which the law tends to look on with disfavor in order to move the rule closer to a system of strict liability. That system ties liability to the application of force in cases of harm between strangers, and to compliance with the rules of the road in highway accidents. All antecedent conduct is presumptively put to one side, except in those emergency settings that constitute a slender portion of the docket. But the critical contrast is this: there is no application of force by an automobile manufacturer whose car is struck in a side collision by a speeding driver long after the manufacturer sold the automobile into the stream of commerce. Nor, to take another example from the law of owner and occupier's liability, has a landlord used

force against a tenant who is physically assaulted on the landlord's premises.[13] In these cases, there are no stops to prevent an excess of discretion
in deciding how much care is reasonably required and how much not.

One way to deal with this problem, of course, is to leave the question of warnings and design to market institutions, such that the consumer bears the risk of obvious dangers, and the manufacturer, landowner, or physician bears the risk of hidden dangers. Yet suppose it is
thought, with some justification, that the line between open and hidden
is not clear enough to bear the full weight of the system, even if it does
supply the neat type of on/off switch that is appropriate for a system of
tort liability. At this point, there is no reason to sacrifice all the rule-of-
law concerns with uniformity and administratability by retreating to the
contours of a general negligence system. The correct *nonmarket* way to
attack this problem is to rely on explicit regulatory standards, known in
advance, to again furnish the clear line between innocent and culpable
conduct that any system of tort liability needs to operate well. Compliance with a known standard easily meets the requirements of the rule of
law. It also allows for uniformity across individual cases, and for a reduction in administrative costs, without undermining the incentives on
all product users to take care in the selection and administration of their
products.

Unfortunately, the current deep-seated institutional players in both
legislatures and courts have led to a total rejection of this norm, with
the consequent expansion of tort liability. Compliance with design or
warning standards is commonly said to set a "minimum standard" of
good conduct, but it is never itself regarded as sufficient to meet the
standard of good conduct.[14] It is a matter of some debate as to the benefit that any defendant gets from compliance with all known standards,
but the bottom line today is that the phrasing of jury instructions does
not matter. Juries have largely unreviewable discretion on this matter, so
that their attitudes toward the businesses and professions sets a standard
of liability that varies enormously across states, counties, and indeed individual courtrooms. Many juries will have more sense than the judges

that confer upon them unbridled discretion. But given the law of large numbers, some juries in big cases will not. The upshot is that huge departures from sensible downstream uses do not result in exoneration for upstream players.

In some cases, the misconduct of the injured party results in a small reduction in the percentages of damages, which is offset by inflating the base figure to begin with. In other cases, the plaintiff may well be an innocent party, but a set of legal maneuvers allows a downstream user in a regime of joint and several liability to use all sorts of tactical maneuvers to switch the costs back to the upstream producer. The most egregious illustration of the pattern arose in the recent Supreme Court decision in *Wyeth v. Levine*,[15] which involved the serious maladministration of the painkiller Phenergan. An instance of mistaken administration of the drug, which had been on the market for over fifty years, resulted in gangrene and amputation of the arm of the plaintiff, a professional musician. The mistake arose when a physician's assistant disregarded a Phenergan warning label that cautioned against an injection of the drug into an artery, which was known to result in a pushback of red blood. The warnings set out both the permissible dosage and the appropriate speed of its injection. The instructions said to use the more dangerous method of the "IV push" of Phenergan into the vein only when the drip method had failed, which it had in this case. The physician's assistant violated every stated precaution, and the predicted gangrene followed. The Vermont Supreme Court held that this conduct could, if a jury so found, give rise to liability of the *manufacturer* under state law, on the ground that a stronger warning might have deterred use of the Phenergan. The United States Supreme Court refused to hold that the detailed and exhaustive FDA warnings "occupied the field" in ways that blocked the state tort law from its operation.

The technical differences of statutory defenses under state law and preemption defenses (in which superior federal laws displace or preempt state laws) are not to the point here. What really matters is the common state of mind that leads to the utter refusal to announce and rely on clear rules in advance. The utter refusal to allow institutional rules to govern the case was, in this instance, a form of judicial lawlessness that offends Fuller's requirements about how a sound legal system should operate. It may seem to be a matter unworthy of serious elaboration to expand the role of reasonableness to these cases of physical harm. But the same notion that functions with tolerable efficiency as a backstop to more specific and knowable rules becomes the source of a massive transformation of liability when, wholly unmoored, it becomes the sole test setting standards of manufacturer or professional liability. The critics who denounce the current systems of liability as a violation of the rule of law are right. The tragedy is that the judges and legislatures who ought to know better shy away from the regime of fixed and known rules that could avoid virtually all of these problems. Major advances in the medical and product fields should have translated into an equally major contraction of liability over the past two generations, and not into the hundred- or thousand-fold expansion of liability that, virtually surreptitiously, has taken place.

3

Where Natural Law and Utilitarianism Converge

Natural Law and Utilitarian Theory

The previous two chapters sought to integrate a number of themes about the relationship of rules to discretion in the administration of a sound legal system. We have already established conceptually how difficult it is to defend a content-free version of the rule of law, or indeed to banish notions of reasonableness or good faith from any legal system. Try as one may, sooner or later the inquiry requires articulation of a substantive theory that addresses three key issues: first, identifying the rights and duties of individuals; second, determining how those rights should be classified for the purposes of various legislative and administrative schemes; and third, identifying at what level discretion must be vested in public officials to make the overall system operable.

In order to answer those questions, we must place an inquiry into the rule of law squarely in a larger context of legal and political theory. If we do this task correctly, then the rule of law falls out of the system as one important constraint on the way in which state power should be properly exerted against various individuals and groups. The basic goal is to articulate how a complete legal system should be developed, in which the rule of law plays a key internal role. In doing this, we should begin with the articulation of substantive rules, a process that then sets the stage for an examination of the principles of sound public administration.

In this regard, the earlier legal systems clearly used the notion of the rule of law to signal the support of some strong system of individual liberty and property rights. No one who studies Roman law or the early English legal materials derived from them could reach a different conclusion on two issues. The first is the key role that the rule of law is thought to play in the organization of the criminal law, where its function is to limit the discretion of public officials. The second is the dominance of private law in the organization of legal systems. The private-law developments are marked by a deep sophistication in stating general rules that are then ingeniously applied to particular problems in the law of property, contract, tort, restitution, and wills. The results are so solid that they have descended in broad outline to the present generation. Yet that early sophistication on principles and cases does *not* carry over to the foundational work supplying, as a matter of first principle, broad normative support to their basic conceptions.

One major purpose of this short book is to bridge that gap between time-honored principles and their theoretical justification. The tools of analysis available today are drawn from both political theory and economics, and allow us to furnish the substructure needed to integrate notions of the rule of law into a larger understanding of both individual rights and social institutions. But all too often, modern political theory does not seek to develop these connections in a systematic way. The discussions of the rule of law are often couched in broad abstractions, with little reference to the internal complexity of both the public and private law. Great writers, such as Friedrich Hayek, have been content to speak at a high level of generality, without drilling down into the details of any legal system. All too often, the jurisprudential literature on the rule of law examines the topic with great fervor, yet with little understanding. It is therefore critical to explore exactly how the two conceptually distinct notions of the rule of law and private property interact in practice. In this chapter, my immediate purpose is to explain, in nontechnical terms, why these twin pillars of classical liberalism should be regarded neither as benign truisms nor as disconnected sentiments. Instead, they should be recognized as the key for generating a sustainable government possessed with the means, and imbued by the ends, needed to create a sustainable free and open society. In order to defend these strong claims, we must examine both the methodological foundations and the substantive choices that give strength to the classical liberal program.

On methodology, what metric should be used to make judgments about desirable social policy? Many small-government libertarians rely on intuitive and immutable conceptions of right and wrong—often traveling under the name of "natural law"—that are said to lead to a powerful conception of autonomy or self-ownership. That invocation of natural-law principles was the dominant mode of argumentation all the way through modern times. Justinian set the tone in his *Institutes,* when he said simply: "The maxims of law are these: to live honestly, to hurt no one, to give every one his due."[1] The hard work comes in the explication of the terms "honestly," "hurt," and "his due." To the natural lawyers, these terms cashed out into a strong prohibition against the use of force and fraud, wholly without regard to the larger social consequences of their widespread use. Small-government libertarians' proposal for a sound legal order thus focuses on the immediate parties. It all too easily ignores the indirect, if substantial, effects—both positive and negative—that their actions have on third parties. The analysis is thus partial and incomplete. The same can be said of the view that all promises should be enforceable, again regardless of their social consequences—a claim that likewise turns out to be overly broad. The repeated emphasis on philosophical intuition in the areas of both coercion and agreement is sometimes backed by some deep trust in the direct perception of right and wrong. These two tools are thought to provide better means of realizing sound political objects than deductive logic, theoretical constructs, or systematic empirical evaluation.

Historically, however, this pat opposition between just acts and desirable consequences does not quite ring true. The English phrase "natural law" does not refer to a comprehensive political theory incubated in an institutional vacuum. The Roman phrase *naturalis ratio,* literally translated, means "the reason of nature," where "reason" stresses the rules of the natural-law theory, and "nature" points to the external world, including physical and biological phenomena, as the stuff on which that theoretical reasoning operates. Therefore, natural law historically stood for the proposition that the rules of social interaction should be conformable to human nature; in other words, the rules should help to bring out the best instincts and actions in all peoples governed by the strictures of natural law.

Unfortunately, incautious biologists often misinterpret this doctrine, making the false claim that whatever people do is natural, and thus right solely because they have done it.[2] But the use of biological data by natural-law theorists working in the Roman tradition was rarely that crude. Rather, many classical natural lawyers believed that the implicit wisdom of natural—or in some cases, divine—law was best evidenced by the salutary effect that these principles had on the communities whose members exhibited a high level of compliance with its dictates.

On this reading, the key switch from natural law to modern forms of consequentialism (a theory based on satisfying human ends or utility) is less dramatic than it first appears. The test of social utility, broadly conceived and imprecisely specified, as in the work of David Hume,[3] no longer counted as mere evidence of some natural or divine order, as it had in the works of earlier theist writers.[4] Instead, social utility became the overarching test by which social institutions were valuated under a natural-law theory. In using the terms "social utility" and "consequentialism," I am not claiming that there is some transcendent utility that exists independent of the welfare of those people who are impacted, positively and negatively, by the choice of legal rules or the behavior of other individuals. I am suggesting only that we judge the merits of the rules by the consequences they have on the individuals they govern. In that sense, unless noted in context, I use the terms "utilitarian" and "consequential" as synonyms, without dwelling on their subtly different shades of meaning.

Measured in utilitarian terms, however, traditional natural-law theories suffer from serious limitations, especially when applied to the complex institutions of the modern administrative state. It is important, however, to first recount the successes of natural law before dwelling on its limitations. As noted above, many natural-law rules can be distilled into two overarching principles: first, prohibit coercion; and second, facilitate cooperation among autonomous individuals. It would, however, be a great mistake to think that these rules exhaust the realm of relevant forms of social control of human interactions, especially in more complex social settings. The tasks for any modern society include taxation, preservation of domestic law and order, national defense, construction of social infrastructure, and control of monopoly power by the use of an antitrust law and/or the regulation of network industries.

Small-Number Disputes

How, then, does one unite the impulses of natural law and those of a more systematic consequentialist theory? The correct analysis starts with the usual two-party situations that characterize most disputes over voluntary contracts and personal wrongs, or torts. The term "two-party situations" should not be taken with excessive literalism, for it is not meant to exclude any transactions that involve a small number of individuals, each of whom is acting typically on his own account. Disputes can arise among three joint owners of property, as well as between two. A contract between A and B can be assigned to C; two persons can combine to injure a third; and so on.

Rules on coercion and cooperation supply a sensible roadmap in these more complex situations by *decomposing* any three-party situation into a set of two-party disputes. In principle—abstracting from the weighty problem of judicial administration—one need only first resolve the dispute between A and B to see which party bears the loss. Once this outcome is determined, the next inquiry examines the claims for redress that the loser of the first dispute—say, B—has against C. The order of analysis does not matter: no matter which of the three pairs is chosen first, the resulting succession of two-party lawsuits should lead ultimately to the same distribution of benefits and losses. Thus, if B loses to A and prevails against C, the hierarchy of responsibility is A > B > C. If the order of suits started with A versus C, A would prevail over C, and C in turn would lose to B. When the maneuvering ceases, the same hierarchy of A > B > C results. The same strategy could apply as additional parties D through Z are introduced into the system. If there are *n* parties, it should always be possible to have *n* − 1 lawsuits to establish a unique hierarchy among the parties. If the rules are consistent, then as a matter of theory the sequence of the pairwise comparisons does not matter.

As a matter of moral theory, the correct result is always strictly hierarchical: hold the most culpable party responsible to the party which is least culpable, ignoring those in the middle. But in a world where some parties are insolvent or beyond the jurisdiction of the courts, the hierarchy has greater significance. For example, on the hypothetical given above, A should be allowed to prevail against B if C is unable to pay any judgment against him. These intermediate judgments are often the most painful to make as a theoretical matter. To present one famous legal triangle, consider the case where A entrusts goods to C, who in turn sells them off without permission to B and then flees with the proceeds of the sale. The easy part of the problem is that C should lose to both A and B. The hard part of the inquiry is to determine whether to allow the original owner, A, to prevail over the purchaser in good faith, B, when C is nowhere to be found.[5]

As a procedural matter, moreover, the addition of any new party creates major stresses on the operation of a procedural system. All of the rules that deal with pleadings, jurisdiction, motions for discovery before trial, joinder of parties, and the conduct of trial and appeal are made far more difficult when three parties are involved instead of the usual two. At this point, the object of the legal system is to devise procedural rules that permit the ascertainment of proper hierarchical order at the lowest possible administrative cost. The alternatives include the development of complex rules for class actions, permissive joinder, and intervention, which necessarily rest in large measure on the sound discretion of trial judges in the conduct of a given case. In general, when courts are asked to manage litigation, they cannot be asked to bring to their delicate task more precision than any private manager can bring to his or her task. The parallels to sound prosecutorial discretion should be evident.

In working out the dynamics of these small-number disputes, the best results are often (as natural lawyers suspected) achieved by rules and practices that *ignore* social consequences to particular parties that flow from deciding individual cases. In many instances, the position goes under the name of "corrective justice," where the task of the legal system is to offer remedies that correct the injustices that one person commits against the other. The focus of any system of corrective justice is on the immediate interaction of the parties, in conscious disregard of other social consequences. The narrowness of the inquiry is what makes it possible to develop moral judgments that can be translated into legal commands. This notion is often associated with Aristotle, who, in dealing with this question, caught the proper mood when he stated that "it makes no difference whether a respectable man defrauds a dishonest one, or the converse; nor whether it is a good or a bad man who has committed adultery; the law only looks to the difference caused by the harm done; and it treats the parties as equals, if one wrongs and the other is wronged, and if one does and the other suffers loss or harm."[6]

The undeniable genius of this simple passage does not lie in how it defines the particular wrongs for which some redress is granted. On that issue, Aristotle's efforts to link the balance in the law to some conception of "arithmetic proportion" is a major analogical failure that has been consigned to the dustbin of intellectual history. What does matter is that he announced in a few sentences the wide range of issues that should be *excluded* from the relevant decisionmaking process, making it possible to confine disputes within well-defined boundaries. The key task is to shrink the field of relevant discourse so that the relevant pairwise comparisons can be made without a detailed inquiry into the nature and origins of the universe.

That same attitude toward the rules of the gains from ordinary exchanges of goods and services can be extended to contracts, even those said to be "in restraint of trade," as the common-law expression puts it.[7] It is not feasible to run a system of contract law by seeking to show on a case-by-case basis that the transaction in question works some kind of social improvement. The correct approach instead obtains that information at far lower cost by looking to the generic features of all voluntary transactions. That is, we know that individuals will normally enter into trade when animated by the prospect of individual gain. Let both sides in a two-party transaction share in that objective, and both sides will be better off than before.

This simple insight is now capable of generalization in two distinct ways. The first is to note that sequential contracts work this way over time, so that if A first deals with B, and then takes the goods received from B to sell to C, we have two positive-sum transactions instead of one. Similarly, if A and B find a reason to include C in their transaction, the mutual-gain condition still applies to three people. Take these two rules and combine them in whatever fashion the parties want, and this recombination then allows the parties to wring a greater amount of social gain out of any fixed set of physical, intellectual, and human re-sources. At this point, the proper technique for advancing social welfare takes a leaf from the great work of Ronald Coase.[8] Reducing friction, or transaction costs, increases the velocity of exchange, and thereby in-creases overall wealth and human satisfaction. Work toward the former, which is measurable, and the latter, which is so hard to measure, will be advanced as if by, to coin a phrase, an invisible hand.

Similar arguments apply, in reverse, to the use of force and fraud. Force and fraud necessarily diminish the wealth of the victim, usually by far more than the gains to the assailant. The diminished wealth among immediate parties to the transaction necessarily reduces the prospects of third persons by cutting off their future opportunities for gains from either trade or cooperation. Again, we do not have to dem-onstrate this proposition on a case-by-case basis in order to reach the right result, which is to curb aggression and to block those agreements that allow individuals to cooperate in ways that reduce overall social welfare. It is for this reason that a contract to kill a third person is now recharacterized as a criminal conspiracy and resale of stolen goods is re-branded as fencing or trafficking. The private gains from these trades are a bad thing, because they result in systemic harms to third persons that diminish overall social utility.

This overall evaluation of social welfare should determine the shape of ordinary litigation. Thus, a private right of action for the injured plaintiff should be structured so that it advances social welfare whenever it advances individual welfare. At this point, the principled genuine dis-putes are not over basic rights and wrongs, but over the choice of reme-dies available to the innocent party. Is self-help allowed, and, if so, how is it limited? Can people obtain protective orders against future abuse, and, if so, how effective will these turn out to be? Can the law refuse to enforce contracts in restraint of trade? A sensible discussion about these hard choices on means arises precisely because of the strong social agree-ments on ends. The entire apparatus is directed toward minimizing the frequency and severity of aggressive and conspiratorial maneuvers. The exercise yields a large social payoff, if only by indirection. Allowing one person to curb the use of force and fraud lets innocent bystanders ride free on his shoulders. As I shall discuss in Chapter 11, this set of insights does not take us all the way there. But by the same token, it so limits the form of discourse that the complex cases of individuated judgments can typically be limited to the small class of emergencies in which one party is put in the unfortunate position of trying to minimize the risks that emerge from the misconduct of others.

This systematic approach allows us to see the differences in social consequences between a regime that fosters cooperation and one that tolerates or assists coercion. The former has positive externalities; the latter has negative ones. This basic conclusion is only reinforced when the prohibition against force and fraud is fleshed out by adding the common defenses to liability, covering issues such as duress and fraud in contract, or assumption of the risk and self-defense in tort. These defenses exhibit the same external effects, for if the defense makes sense in any dispute between two parties, it also makes sense from the vantage point of third parties. Most disputes involving breach of contract and physical injuries can be resolved economically in ways that advance social welfare, *without* requiring us to wear our utilitarian credentials on our sleeves. It is therefore possible for nonconsequentialists operating in the natural-law tradition to gravitate toward rules that lead to the right decisions, even if they have no idea of how to make the correct social calculations.[9]

At this point it becomes possible to understand the implicit good sense behind two expressions, one legal and the other economic, that limit the potential scope of liability: *damnum absque iniuria* and "pecuniary externality." Unfortunately, both of these terms have generated their fair share of linguistic and intellectual confusion. The first, which carries over into modern times from the Roman law, means "harm without legal injury." The latter is a parallel modern economic expression, which refers to adverse effects on strangers that ought to be ignored in setting out the social calculus. For these purposes, the Wikipedia definition works just fine: "A pecuniary externality is an externality which operates through prices rather than through real resource effects. For example, an influx of city-dwellers buying second homes in a rural area can drive up house prices, making it difficult for young people in the area to get onto the property ladder." This is in contrast to "technical externalities" or "real externalities," which have a direct resource effect on a third party. For example, pollution from a factory directly harms the environment. Pecuniary externalities should not be taken into account in cost-benefit analysis.[10]

Why, quite simply, aren't both of these conceptions double talk? Why aren't all harms also injuries in line with John Stuart Mill's harm principle? "[T]he sole end for which mankind are warranted, individually or collectively, in interfering with the liberty of action of any of their number is self-protection. The only purpose for which power can rightfully be exercised over any member of a civilised community against his will, is to prevent harm to others."[11] What counts as a pecuniary externality anyhow? And why should pecuniary externalities be ignored when real externalities are taken into account?

The answers to these questions lie in understanding the relationship between private rights of redress on the one hand, and background principles of social welfare on the other. In principle, a legal system should not remedy harms that are *inversely* correlated with overall social welfare. Put otherwise, negative external effects must be offset by private gains to the parties involved. In those cases where private gains are systematically larger, courts should not allow the private action. For example, look at the two leading instances of *damnum absque iniuria:* first, the blocking of your view by your neighbor's new construction, and, second, losing your customers to a competitor who offers lower prices or superior service, or both. Both losses reduce the value of land to an individual landowner just as if his property had been burnt to the ground or his customers had been forcibly driven away from his place of business. But the social consequences diverge once all third-party effects are taken into account. As I discuss more fully later, blocked views mean that others get to build, while competition between vendors increases choices to third persons; both are social gains.

Against this backdrop, the central task of any sound liberal order is to *prevent* disappointed neighbors and competitors from obtaining relief against new entrants through either the courts or the legislature. The inability to do this will lead to the strangulation of development and trade. Precisely this happens when zoning boards are allowed to delay or reconfigure, seemingly without limit, new projects that alter the relative property values in a neighborhood, which such projects always do. And the results are the same whenever new competitors are required to first obtain state permits solely because they reduce the value of established businesses, which again, new competitors always do.

The protection of private property and the safeguarding of economic liberties are the essential hallmarks of a strong classical liberal system, because the third-party effects of these protections are always positive. Unfortunately, "protectionism" against new rivals offers a seductive imitation of the protection of private property and economic liberty. But it is a perversion of the noble classical liberal ideal, because the third-party effects of protectionist activities are always negative. In the language of modern game theory, competition and development generate *positive*-sum games for all individuals in society; restriction and coercion lead to *negative*-sum games for the same people. We want to play the former as often as possible, and the latter as infrequently as possible. In that stark contrast lies the good sense in the twin mysterious conceptions of *damnum absque iniuria* and pecuniary externalities. And such principles show how natural law theory, in its most sensible formulation, converges with a sensible version of utilitarian theory. The successes of the older systems of the law on the ground were not the result of happenstance. They were the result of the durable good economic sense of these substantive rules. The time has now come to examine the more systematic divergence between natural-law and utilitarian conceptions in large social contexts.

4

Where Natural Law and Utilitarianism Diverge

In the previous chapter, I tried to identify the correlation between natural law and social welfare. But that coincidence does break down in some critical cases. To give but one example, let's return to the amorphous category of contracts in restraint of trade. In this area, a natural-law theory based on libertarian principles has *nothing to say* about their distinctive character. It cannot isolate any relevant difference between cartels that fix prices, limit output, and divide territories, on the one hand, and predation on the other, where it is alleged (but rarely if ever proved) that one firm has lowered its prices to drive competitors out of business, in order to recoup gains by charging monopoly prices down the road.[1] The obvious use of predator/prey analogies from the world of nature, red in tooth and claw, does not carry over to the economic universe, where these more elemental weapons have already been removed from the fray.

Deprived of these dubious analogies, the die-hard libertarian faces a theoretical problem: there is no way to distinguish between these two situations, because neither involves the use of force, or any breach of contract. Yet the basic principles of modern economics can help to explain the sharp difference between the two types of cases. The predation strategies simply don't allow the supposed predators to vanquish their foes. The firm that cuts prices today has to contend with a flood of additional demand at a price below cost. Yet it will rarely be in a position to recoup these losses down the road, as fresh entrants can always enter to bid future prices down to a competitive level. Given the tendency of predation schemes to overshoot the mark, the great risk here is that the antitrust laws will be used to block legitimate moves that firms use to lower prices to sustainable competitive levels, where the possibility of recoupment is irrelevant.

In contrast, cartel arrangements pose very different challenges to social welfare. Left to their own devices, cartels are sustainable for some indefinite period of time. These arrangements raise prices above the competitive level and generate gains to producers that are smaller than the losses to consumers in both the short and the long run. Any exchange that would have occurred somewhere between the competitive price and the monopoly price will no longer occur after the price increase. The social loss is undeniable, but difficult to quantify. The key question is how to compare the administrative costs of combating monopolies with the allocative gains of limiting their impact. The empirical evidence can cut both ways, so a compromise position that will expose some cartels makes sense even if others slip through the net.

I leave those difficult choices to one side, because that level of intellectual refinement is never necessary to condemn the expanding class of *state-created* monopolies. One familiar example is the collective-bargaining regime that the New Deal imposed on labor markets;[2] another covers the marketing orders used to restrict output in agricultural goods.[3] In both settings, the administrative costs of cartel creation are an essential part of the social losses that these schemes create. Since both components of cartel formation—administrative cost increases and negative external effects—are negative, their sum is necessarily negative as well. As such, in this context it is always unnecessary to determine their relative magnitudes, given that their sum is necessarily a larger negative. Two negatives are always greater than one, so the state should *never* embark on these dangerous, if well-entrenched, ventures. In assessing these larger projects, however, natural-law theory, which was developed in a very different intellectual milieu, comes up short because its libertarian backdrop does not differentiate contracts into their appropriate subclasses. Indeed, it is hard to think of any major progressive "reform" of the New Deal period that did not serve to shore up cartels by restricting entry into critical product and labor markets.[4]

Pareto versus Kaldor-Hicks

The stark libertarian approach also falls short because it does not explain why the state has the power to tax individuals who have committed no wrongs and who have made no promises. Simply stating a generalized preference for a limited government does not answer the hard question of how limited that government should be and why. Accordingly, a sound libertarian system quietly morphs into classical liberalism on key matters of restraint of trade, taxation, and eminent domain. At this juncture, it becomes imperative to articulate a more systematic way to analyze the costs and benefits of different social arrangements.

That task requires articulating a good definition for "naturalist ethics," in order to link together social desirability and individual desires.[5] The connection between desired and desirable works tolerably well for explaining why something is good for the individual who desires it. What one desires is desirable. There may be some doubts about persons with diseases or diminished capacity, but those details don't matter for organizing large social structures. On matters of political theory, the simple query is: What other test is there anyhow? But it works less well to explain how to deal with the common situations where a single state of affairs is desired by A but opposed by B. The key intellectual move, therefore, is to figure out ways to *combine* these irreducible individual preferences in a nonarbitrary fashion while respecting that, for good reasons of their own, some people want things that others do not.

At this juncture, two economic tests present two related ways to link subjective preferences to social welfare, without having to make utility into some dominant principle that somehow objectively limits the class of permissible choices. The first test is that of Pareto superiority, with its related notion of Pareto optimality. Socially, system A is preferred to system B where at least one person is better off under system A than system B, and no person is worse off in system A than in system B. A Pareto-superior transaction is one that leaves at least one individual better off without making any other individual worse off. Under the Pareto-superior test, these transactions, whether voluntary or forced, should be allowed to continue until the system reaches a Pareto-optimal distribution. A Pareto-optimal distribution is one in which no one can be made better off without making someone else worse off.

The Pareto-superior result can be routinely achieved by introducing new arrangements that improve overall social welfare, without costly side payments among individuals. These arrangements work, so long as the new packets of entitlements generated by legal change are worth more to *every one* of their holders than the existing packets that were taken away. Stressing these forms of *in-kind compensation*—one bundle of property rights is exchanged for another—also avoids the more cumbrous process of requiring each forced change of individual legal rights to be offset by cash compensation, so long as every regulated party is at least as well off after the coercion as before. The great advantage of this system is that if the relevant actors all stand in the same relative positions before and after the change, we can be confident that all have gained—indeed gained in roughly equal proportions—even if we cannot put a monetary value on the changes in question. Thus, a rule that requires all real estate transactions to be evidenced in writing so increases the security of transactions that from the ex ante perspective it is hard to think that anyone loses from the rule, which has endured through thick and thin in virtually every legal system around the world. That judgment stands even though, to this very day, it is difficult for anyone to monetize the system-wide gains in the operation of the real estate market.

The alternative to Pareto superiority is the Kaldor-Hicks approach, in which one system is preferred to another if the gainers in the first system are *hypothetically* able to compensate the losers from that system with their winnings and still remain better off than before. There is no accompanying obligation to make the payments. It is only necessary to identify possible payments that meet that condition. The Kaldor-Hicks approach thus eliminates the administrative burdens that come with running a system that relies on compensation in either cash or kind.

One advantage of the Kaldor-Hicks criterion, therefore, is that it is less demanding than the earlier Pareto tests, which require actual compensation in cash or kind. This advantage plays out in some circumstances where property rights are highly diffuse, so that it is difficult to figure out who should pay whom, even when large increases in social wealth are accompanied by small losses to some determinate class of individuals. It is better that the legislative initiative should go forward, even if those small losses remain uncompensated. Yet it should not be thought that this one consideration shows some uniform dominance for that Kaldor-Hicks formula. Indeed, for a variety of institutional and normative reasons, the end-state envisioned under the Kaldor-Hicks test often is *more* problematic than the exacting end-state under the Paretian test. The key difference is the moral uneasiness and political dynamic unleashed by a Kaldor-Hicks test through its acceptance of a skewed distribution of gains and losses that derive from state action, so long as the subjective gains of the winners exceed the subjective losses to the losers. That imbalance often leads to systematic political strife, as the losers throw every political obstacle in the path of a social improvement that leaves them worse off than before. Compensation in these settings defangs the opposition and thus eases the transition from the less to the more desirable state.

For these purposes, however, I do not wish to dwell on the real institutional differences between normative regimes that require either actual or hypothetical compensation. To the contrary, for some purposes, it is critical *not* to overstate the opposition between the two tests. The Kaldor-Hicks test shares with the Pareto system its robust unambiguous condemnation of *all* systems that *reduce* overall welfare, subjectively measured, whether or not compensation is paid. Neither system has any tolerance for *negative*-sum games. This relationship thus ties into our earlier discussion of the relationship between competitive and monopoly markets, because any state-mandated movement from competitive markets to monopolistic ones is characterized by a net decrease of social output, which condemns it under *both* the Pareto and Kaldor-Hicks standards. In other words, the major New Deal programs of the 1930s and their modern parallels flunk both tests.

The choice between these compensation systems is also directly relevant to the legitimate scope of state power. One of the central differences between the pure libertarian system and the classical liberal system lies in the willingness of the classical liberal to tolerate forced exchanges initiated by the use of state power, so long as the party from whom private property is taken receives just compensation from the state. Under the more restrictive libertarian position, by contrast, these forced exchanges tend to be categorically condemned, wholly without regard to the level of compensation offered. Indeed, in some cases we can propose a still more *exacting* standard of social welfare that builds on an intuitive notion of individual fairness. Under that theory, it is not enough for each individual to be left better off by the social change. In addition, each must be made better off in the same degree, so that all gains from the venture are prorated in accordance with the level of investments made.

Any systematic account of state power requires some use of all three tests of social welfare in different contexts. In no case should we want to adopt projects that flunk the Kaldor-Hicks test, whereby the total output is less than it was before the change was initiated. Where possible, we should like to meet the Pareto test to make sure that no individual is disadvantaged by a general social improvement. And finally, if possible, the levels of social stability will be increased if there is a proportionate division of the gain that commends itself to all persons who are made participants in the project. The Pareto test leads to political wrangling over the division of social surplus from worthwhile government projects that a unique and proportional distribution of the gains is able to avoid. For the moment, however, the choice among the approaches is less important than it seems. Substantively, the government programs that I examine on such key topics as agriculture, zoning, environmental protection, and labor markets are negative-sum and thus flunk all three tests. Methodologically, all three of these tests share one key feature: they are strictly *reductionist,* in that they all offer an explicit test for aggregating unbounded subjective individual preferences into social choices. The strong sense of individual autonomy and entitlement to particular endowments gives way, but only in a regime that indicates that all persons count uniformly in the social calculus.

The Social Democratic Alternative

The question is how this approach stacks up against its main competitor: the modern, social democratic, administrative state. The social democratic model rejects a system of limited government grounded in the strong enforcement of both property rights and contract rights. This vision of the modern state should not be confused, of course, with tyrannical efforts to subject all individuals to arbitrary government power. Rather, in its most attractive form, the social democratic model displaces strong individual rights with the creation of a legal regime that, at its best, ensures the participation of all interested persons and groups in an open, deliberative process.[6] The implementation of these collective programs is entrusted to individuals who have technical skills and professional government expertise, and whose power is backed by courts with a willingness to give broad deference to administrative actions that often abridge both property rights and contract rights.[7] This modern administrative synthesis is wrong in both its points. The supposed level of expertise that is involved in many technical activities generally does not extend to the most controversial decisions made in administrative law settings. What is often critical is setting the applicable standard for permissible conduct, and this cannot be done correctly if the entire system works from flawed premises that make entire lines of inquiry irrelevant. A general system of rent control makes no sense in competitive markets, so it offers no consolation that a supposed expert board makes these determinations while going off on a fool's errand. Even in those cases where some administrative decision is needed, as with setting relevant pollution standards, bias can easily negate any supposed expertise. The danger with administrative agencies is that their members are selected for one and only one class of cases. Hence, it is easy to staff these bodies with people who have strong antecedent views that take, for example, the position of management or labor, landlord or tenant, firm or investor. Courts whose judges have to face a wide range of different issues may in fact carry less baggage to any particular dispute.

In addition, it is easy to overestimate the gains from public deliberation on administrative decisions. In this regard, everything depends on the framework of entitlements in which deliberation takes place. It is, for example, clear that all private firms prize some level of deliberation by members of their board of directors on matters that affect the corporation. There are, of course, strong disagreements that will arise about the proper strategies for corporate success. But the key point is that, over a broad range of activity, there is a suitable alignment of interest among the various parties. As a first approximation, no individual director or shareholder makes money when the corporation loses money, regardless of the size of his or her stake. The first-level incentives, therefore, are for honest presentation of information in the hope of improving overall corporate value. To be sure, some shareholders might not have the incentive to invest in gathering information at private expense for the benefit of the firm. But by the same token, the firm itself can commission the studies it needs to make its key decisions. There are, inevitably, situations where the interests of board members clash with those of a corporation, which is why compensation rules are structured to tie the success of the individual officer to the success of the firm, and why self-dealing rules lead to increased scrutiny of certain transactions.

Unfortunately, these business constraints do not work in the political arena, because the interests of the relevant voters do not line up with overall social welfare. The local government that considers restrictions on new development of property owned by outsiders knows that, under current law, it will not have to compensate those parties for the heavy economic losses they will suffer through administrative regulation. At this point, deliberation magnifies the errors in the basic political structure. It is easy to persuade other voters to impose these restrictions, given that the large losses are borne by outsiders. We are then left with the types of political posturing and grandstanding that are part and parcel of these activities. The blunt truth is that political deliberation is no better than the institutional structure in which it is embedded.

By casting its lot with expertise and deliberation, the modern administrative state inverts the relationship between individual rights and political power. The classical liberal theory sees limited government as a means to defend the fundamental rights of property and contract. The modern democratic state, by contrast, defines itself in opposition to any theory of natural law that posits these individual "prepolitical" entitlements as existing prior to the creation of the state. Instead, property rights are arbitrary assemblages of rights which the state creates for its own instrumental purposes, and which it can undo almost at will for the same instrumental ends.

The administrative state also seeks to preserve the rule of law even after it denies the primacy of private property and of freedom of contract. These tensions play out differently from nation to nation, and from subject area to subject area. No one person can hope to master their full complexities. But even after the limitations are acknowledged, it is possible to draw some systematic conclusions. My central thesis is that the modern system of administrative governance is inferior to the more modest and more focused classical liberal system that it displaces, as judged under any of the three standards of social welfare set out above. Stated otherwise, the Kaldor-Hicks, Pareto, and proportionate-gain standards all point in the same direction: against the administrative state.

The secret of good government is to select a few key tasks and to perform those well. To expand beyond these core functions will invariably reduce the overall efficiency of government actions. One illustration is the array of ambitious regulations from the Securities and Exchange Commission (SEC) for dealing with information flows between brokerage houses and their largest customers. Despite these efforts, the SEC still failed to pick up Bernard Madoff's $50 billion fraud. Another example is how the local government's land use agenda, with a strong devotion to affordable-housing programs, can choke off the supply of housing and decimate the tax base into the bargain. Worse still is how the current permit culture allows public administrators to stop construction of new projects no matter how much private labor has been invested in plans. The uncertainty of arbitrary and politically motivated reversals slows down development and raises costs, without producing any structures better than those that private architects can devise. The scarce public resources poured into high-powered determinations of the administrative state are better spent on picking up the garbage from public streets. After all, resources for state enforcement are as scarce as they are everywhere else.

Failure to recognize these political risks has two negative consequences. First, it invites the government to intrude on matters where it would be well advised to stay its hand, such as regulating the wages and hours in ordinary labor contracts. Second, it *weakens* the effectiveness of government in those areas—such as the control of force and fraud—where its core political responsibilities lie.

The shift to large government programs in the United States derives from the progressive agenda of the first third of the twentieth century, which set out the blueprint for Franklin Roosevelt's New Deal.[8] In order to defend the superiority of the classical liberal model, I shall first set out the traditional understanding of the relationship between the rule of law and private property. Thereafter, I shall discuss the modern version of that relationship, in order to explain how the breakdown of old restraints has led to serious government dysfunctions in a wide range of substantive areas.

5

Property Rights in the Grand Social Scheme

What We Mean by Private Property

The previous chapters have shown how even the thinnest conception of the rule of law helps to prevent the corruption that can result from the unlimited discretion of law enforcement officials. The basic protections of neutral judges, notice of charges, and an opportunity to be heard are minimum conditions for any sound legal system.

But are they sufficient? Let us begin with one common source of uneasiness with a limited conception of the rule of law. Any possible gain from complying with these procedural safeguards is precarious because the noblest procedures can be placed in the service of the most odious political agendas. If all that mattered were faithful adherence to formal norms, a Nazi state could properly make it a crime for Jews to engage in commerce, and punish them to the limits of the law if they disobeyed. This legal rule would be acceptable, so long as any litigation to enforce it met the appropriate civil constraints on burdens of proof, right to jury trial, and the like, which is easy to do. The only way to counteract this selective legislation on rule-of-law grounds is through the adoption of a strong neutrality norm or nondiscrimination provision, substantive in nature, which holds that the government cannot favor members of one religion over another, or members of some religion over nonbelievers. These rules have some real advantages insofar as they make it difficult for the government to attack one group containing its opponents unless it is prepared to attack a second, containing its supporters. The antidiscrimination law thus holds one's friends hostage in dealings with one's enemies. The rules work quite well, for example, when the only way to tax your opponents is to tax your supporters. But in some instances, these rules will fall short, for it is quite possible that the activities taxed are critical to the economic survival of your opponents, but not to you or your supporters. The *disparate impact* of a neutral rule could thus be quite devastating.

Everyone accepts that some nondiscrimination norm is part of the rule of law. But in many instances, the more forthright and defensible position is to obviate the problem by linking, as Fuller himself recognized, the procedural component of the rule of law to a sound version of individual rights, so that there is an independent normative case for the faithful enforcement of the legal rules. The nondiscrimination provision counts as one such effort because it means that the dominant faction must subject itself to the same limitations that it wishes to impose on other groups. This principle has a central role to play in any comprehensive system of laws that protects private property and personal liberties. But it does not offer to either property or liberty a preferred position because of its inherent desirability.

It is instructive to then ask how a sound system of individual rights interacts with the rule of law. For most analytical purposes, these two notions should be treated as part of one comprehensive theme, as they were in Locke's famous formulation of property that spoke of "lives, liberties, and estates."[1] Locke's phrase has a profound echo in the Due Process Clauses of the Fifth and Fourteenth Amendments of the United

States Constitution, which protect all persons against the deprivation of "life, liberty or property, without Due Process of Law," whether done by the national government or the states. From this point forward, I shall concentrate on how these protections play out with economic growth and prosperity. But it is important to remember, quite simply, that there is no area of human activity to which the generalized principles of liberty and property are irrelevant. There is nothing about the principle of property that requires individuals to exclude everyone from their lands, even if they are entitled to do so as a matter of right. An individual can devote his land to whatever purposes he sees fit. Similarly, and for the same reasons, there is nothing about the logic of contract that requires all individuals to become entrepreneurs if they are more comfortable with taking positions with lower risk and lower returns. There is nothing about the logic of contract that makes everyone duty-bound to achieve gains from their transactions. Individuals can enter into agreements that contain some overt or disguised gift component. The expression that all contracts reflect, in Thomas Hobbes's famous word, the "appetite" of the parties should not be interpreted as insisting that all appetites are arbitrary, when many can be refined or generous.[2] The strength of the contractual system is that it allows freedom of choice as to ends. The familiar reference to profit or gain reflects only the undeniable truth that in most transactions mutual gain, whether pecuniary or reputational, is the object of both parties.

The ownership of private property, and the labor used for productive purposes, are our most pervasive social institutions. But to understand how they function, we must first disabuse ourselves of the notion that these rights must be absolute in form and content just because they are important. That caricature appeals most to the critics of private property rights.[3] But it amounts to a crude *reductio ad absurdum* that ignores all of the nuances found in a sound system of private property. It is therefore important to see why this absolutist conception of private property goes astray within the classical liberal system in order to set up a more measured defense of a system of strong, but not absolute, property and contract rights.

Common Property

The first objection to the absolutist notion starts with the simple observation that all societies, from ancient times to the present, have had to make room for common property. Rivers and oceans and beaches are there for all to use and for none to appropriate privately.[4] That one simple rule made it possible in ancient times, as it does today, to develop transportation and communication networks that cannot be blocked by each and every property owner along the way.[5] Every modern society has, as one of its core missions, the preservation and maintenance of these common networks. But it is important to make sure that the governing rules are not tilted in a fashion that favors, for example, early comers over late arrivals in determining access to the network. To do otherwise is to encourage people to stake out excessive claims early on, solely to preserve their tactical advantages over latecomers.

The difference between land and water leads instructively to a clear reversal of property rules. Historically, "Prior in time is higher in right" was the maxim that established priority of rights over those things that could be reduced to private ownership: land, animals, and chattels. But that rule is the antithesis of any system that seeks to harmonize use of a commons, for in this case early use is routinely condemned as jumping the gun—a premature effort to secure a disproportionate use of a common resource. Thus, if an electrical grid serving a neighborhood has limited capacity, the first to build cannot gobble up all its capacity to the exclusion of the latecomers.[6] The proper rule allows interim use of the grid until those latecomers arrive, at which point the initial users have to scale back to their pro rata share in the expanded pool. There is no other way to prevent strategic overconsumption.

A similar issue arises with various forms of monopoly. In many cases, the best solution to deal with monopolization is to prevent the merger of two firms that could exert that kind of market power. But in some industries, the monopoly is created for good reason by statute. One familiar instance is the government customs house, which is used to store goods meant for sale overseas, while insulating them free of local taxes. The creation of a single outlet is (or at least was) necessary for goods meant for the foreign trade. The same problem arises in more complex form with network industries. Briefly stated, these are industries that operate to connect parties by network elements such as roads, wires, pipes, and rails, which are always long and thin. One general characteristic of these industries is that it is often costly to build parallel systems, so that the owner of one comprehensive system manages to obtain a natural monopoly—one that is not dependent on government protection from new entry—that allows him to reduce output and charge supracompetitive prices. Dealing with a natural monopoly creates two opposite risks: monopolization by the firm, and confiscation by its government regulator.

In this environment, the law has tried to split the difference. It has held that the monopolist cannot charge whatever price the market will bear. Instead, firms are limited to charging reasonable and nondiscriminatory (RAND) rates. That rule is not intended to deny the monopolist a competitive return on his investment, but is meant to deny him the right to play favorites among customers, which could distort the competitive balance among network users.

Unfortunately, the formulas used to achieve this result leave much to be desired. The problem is not as easy as it is with the customs house, whose rates are benchmarked by the rates that ordinary warehouses charge in a competitive market. Network industries cannot rely on some competitive yardstick. Instead, the rates have to be constructed. In some cases, the rate-making system offers a high rate of return only to those elements that are actually used in running the system. In other cases, the rate regulation offers a lower rate of return on all the capital invested in the business, whether productive or not.[7] One critical danger with all systems of rate regulation is that the promotion of short-run (static) efficiency stifles long-run (dynamic) efficiency, a situation that arises when new technology innovations upset existing business practices.[8] The firm that knows that its return is secure is likely to do less well in the managing of its resources in the long run.[9] Trading off between these two forms of efficiency is an uncertain and unsatisfying process. It is important, moreover, to recognize that the peculiar features of some industries may make rate-making more tractable in those industries than in others. Rate regulation works better with slower-moving technologies like electrical transmission, where static elements dominate, than for faster-moving ones like telecommunications or the Internet, where dynamic elements loom larger.

Historically, the regulated firms were said, with some loss in precision, to be "affected with the public interest."[10] The control of monopoly pricing was, moreover, not the only risk. Since there was no competitive benchmark, as there was in the customs house case, aggressive legislators and administrators could turn the entire process into a disguised act of confiscation by setting rates so low that the regulated business could not earn a decent rate of return on its invested capital. All government need do is allow rates that permit the firm to recover a bit more than its variable costs of operation. At that juncture, the firm will not leave the business, even though it can never make a profit on its initial investment. Other investors will get the message and will refuse to invest today in projects that yield only a positive rate of return tomorrow. To forestall that risk, courts imposed constitutional protections against unduly low rates; without such protections, future investment cycles would never take place, given the justified fears of expropriation.

The choice of regulatory design matters enormously in promoting the efficiency of the system. Here is one modern example. The basic design features of the 1996 Telecommunications Act[11] show how easy it is for regulation to fall off the trolley. The Federal Communications Commission (FCC) is in charge of organizing the telecommunications system, so that separate firms can be linked together in ways that allow the customers of any given firm to reach the customers of all other firms on the network. Two strategies for achieving this linkage are possible. The first requires interconnecting with existing carriers at reasonable rates. This approach imposes on new entrants the cost of building up a new network or adapting an old one for new uses. The social downside of this approach is that it requires new entrants to build out duplicative networks. The alternative approach avoids this problem by allowing new entrants to cannibalize key network elements from incumbent carriers. The downside here is that the FCC must figure out how to set the prices at which these elements can be acquired.

In 1996, the build-out option looked unattainable for telecommunications systems except at prohibitive cost. But that turned out to be an illusion, as new technologies (think of VoIP) allowed the adaptation of existing networks at low prices. Choosing the second approach, the forced sale of unbundled network elements (UNEs) thus turned out to be a huge mistake that foundered on the valuation problem. The FCC ordered the incumbent carriers to supply UNEs to new entrants at below-market prices. The Supreme Court sustained its order by deferring to the agency.[12] The upshot was massive overclaiming of these elements by new firms, whose combined demands prevented the incumbent carriers from ever recovering their historical costs over the life of their assets. Yet at the same time, the new entrants failed to gain a permanent foothold because they competed away the UNE subsidy given to all, so that they, too, ended up losing money during the process.

Requiring incumbent carriers to interconnect with new entrants that built their own networks also involves the use of state coercion, but it leaves far less discretion to the state, if only because there is an easy focal point, whereby no cash changes hands in either direction, for making the linkage under a "bill and keep" regime. That rule worked well for linkages between two land line telephone companies. Back in 1996, however, the same technique could not work for cell phone connections, given the high cost of cell line connections. But relatively simple lump-sum transfer payments could have solved that problem until, as is now the case, the costs of the two systems converged.

Ironically, many of the future trends in telecommunications were not foreseen in 1996, when the well-nigh universal assumption was that land lines would continue to dominate the system. Needless to say, that prediction proved woefully wrong. The use of land lines has contracted, while that of cell phones has expanded. The lesson is to adopt the form of regulation that is likely to prove robust against rapid transitions in technology, which are easy to foresee, as it were, in retrospect.

Separate Property

Much—probably most—productive property, of course, is embodied not in networks but in tangible objects that are capable of being reduced to private ownership. It is at this point that the Roman and common-law conceptions of private property—which have much in common—come into their own. It is critical to note at the outset that the creation of private property that binds all individuals is necessarily *social* at its core. Coercion must replace consent to get the system up and running. Consistent with this vision, the first element of private-property rights in particular things is that these rights are always good *against the world,* wholly without the consent of any other individuals. Without this legal structure, it would not be possible to create secure entitlements in land, structures, equipment, or indeed any form of personal property. Without this condition, the property holder would need to obtain unanimous consent from all living and unborn persons, which is just not feasible in light of the prohibitive transaction costs attendant on such a vainglorious enterprise. Indeed, without some bedrock conception of self-ownership, no individual could claim to be the owner of himself or herself; no one would be in a position to bargain with anyone else to secure his own bodily protection. Nor would any individual have the right to acquire ownership of external things by "occupation," taking *unilaterally* the first possession of otherwise unowned objects, to the exclusion of other possible owners.

Put otherwise, the traditional rule "Prior in time is higher in right"— which has no place at all in regimes of common property—historically became the *sole* means to establish initial ownership rights in private property that was treated as unowned in the state of nature. After all, if the first possessor of an unowned object cannot reduce it to ownership, no one else—certainly not the second possessor—can do so either. The use of this simple rule for ownership is the only way to avoid incurring the prohibitive transaction costs of trying to set out a regime of property rights through universal consent. The human population is in constant flux; the use of agreements to create stable entitlements could not survive the constant birth and death of other individuals.

Just what bundle of rights does private property give to its owner? At this point, it is necessary to loop back to the earlier discussion of Locke and Fuller's view on natural, or procedural, justice. The key insight here is that rights themselves have to be defined in ways that allow them, consistent with rule-of-law principles, to be known and observed by all other individuals with whom no personal communication is possible. The choice of a sound property "baseline" in the original position is not random. Quite the opposite—it is here that the indissoluble empirical connections between property rights and the rule of law are forged. The central proposition is this: the *only* set of substantive rules that achieves that goal is one that requires all persons to *forbear* from interfering with the property rights of any other person, where "interfering" is narrowly defined to involve taking, using, handling, or breaking the property of another. Properly understood, this regime meets all of Fuller's requirements of the rule of law by virtue of its simplicity, coherence, accessibility, and enforceability.

To see why, note the functions served when the legal focus is on forbearance against physical interference.

First, that right is *scalable*. The same configuration of rights can work with a society of 100 acquaintances, or with one of a billion strangers, or anywhere in between. No matter who comes and goes, the maxim "Keep your hands to yourself" remains so clear and salient that everyone can comply, regardless of the diversity in their ethnic backgrounds or personal moral codes.

Second, these rights are *insensitive* to variations in individual or social wealth: the behaviors needed to secure compliance with the basic legal norm of forbearance are attainable in all societies, whether rich or poor. In this regard, traditional property rights differ strongly from modern positive rights to jobs, housing, or health care. Those positive rights can never assume and hold a constant form, for they are always dependent on the ever-changing resource base of society, and on political decisions as to how those resources are to be divided. Standard property rights are not contingent upon overall levels of wealth or technological progress. The basic rights are not in need of constant revision or updating through a collective political process as a society increases or decreases in wealth.

What does change are the uses that people make of their initial endowments, be it through consumption or savings on the individual level, or partnership or exchange on the cooperative level. Those transformations depend in part on consumption decisions, and in part on the individual contracts that property owners (including all people treated as owners of their own labor) make with others from their secure baseline of rights. These contracts can be made, of course, separately and independently in private settings. Each contracting pair can go its own way without creating collective convulsions of the sort that break down under the weight of the more complicated regime of positive rights, which are not easily sustainable in the face of constant changes (often for the worse) in overall wealth or other social conditions. Put otherwise, incremental change is far more likely to proceed in an orderly fashion under a universal system of negative rights—with universal forbearance setting the stage for voluntary exchange—than under any positive-rights regime that purports to supply, say, universal health care.

It is for this reason that the operative principles of an older system of property rights work equally well in ancient and modern societies. Those principles also work equally well in different parts of the globe. It is no accident, therefore, that the standard Roman-law solutions to basic legal problems of tangible property survived with only modest changes until modern times. The natural lawyers built better than they knew. Nor is it an accident that the German Civil Code of 1900, based on Roman principles, could be imported wholesale into Japan, which was governed by wildly different social and cultural norms. A system of property rights that requires only uniform forbearance from the use of force and fraud is effective precisely because it is inconspicuous, easily generalizable, and easily transferrable. It is now critical to explore the bundle of rights in private property.

6

The Bundle of Rights

Composing the Bundle

The topic of this chapter is straightforward enough: What rights does a property owner enjoy against the rest of the world? One element, of course, is the right to *exclude* all other individuals from the ability to enter the owner's property. Clearly if others can enter and take the property for their own use, all rights of any owner are gone. But the right to exclude is not the sole right associated with property ownership.

A second stick in the bundle of rights, which is easy to forget, is the right to enter one's own property. This is distinct from the right to exclude others, and is manifestly necessary in order to allow the owner to gain any enjoyment of his or her property. Once entry is allowed, should the law give the owner the other sticks over the same natural resource? That is, should the law offer any protection to an owner against lesser infringements of property that compromise only the owner's rights to use, sell, or otherwise dispose of the property? The short answer is that it has to. Any robust conception of property rights has to accept the classical liberal legal bundle that includes for everyone the exclusive rights to *occupy, use,* and *dispose* of their property. In addition (and this is an important detail), ownership of land carries with it the right to gain access to the communication and transportation networks, discussed above, that link private owners together and permit them to enjoy the gains from trade.

Putting the rights in this form is meant to dispel the notion that any particular element in this indissoluble bundle enjoys some logical priority over any other element. That deep and uniform conception of the property bundle is indispensable for wringing out the full value of all resources subject to private ownership. To see why, think of a world where the initial property rights contained only one or two elements from this bundle, but not the others. That division of rights would prevent most useful economic activities from ever getting done because of the high transactional barriers that are necessarily erected when different incidents of ownership of the same resource are placed in different hands.

Assume, for the sake of argument, that an owner had only exclusive occupation of some designated land. How could the "owner" of that stripped-down bundle decide to clear or cultivate the land or build improvements on it? Occupation, after all, means only the right to sit on the property; it does not confer the right to use or develop it. Just how are these use and development rights unlocked, if indeed they are to be unlocked at all? One wholly unsatisfactory solution is to say that the approval of everyone else is needed to unleash these rights, at which point we recreate the insoluble transactional obstacles that led to the creation of property rights in the first place. Alternatively, the right to use and develop property could be conditional upon the approval of the state, which can grant or withhold it at will. Yet by that account, the veto power of the public (whose legitimate collective control over any resource is by no means established) could easily block the development of new projects of great value not only to the property's owner, but also to those parties who might wish to deal with him. And exactly that occurs routinely under today's endurance contests that pass for zoning and other forms of land use review. The denial of the right-to-build limits the options of all prospective purchasers. Alternatively, the revised conception of private property could vest some use rights in one individual, and other use rights in other individuals. But this fragmentation of rights accomplishes nothing beyond creating mutual veto powers, which ensure that the value of the whole is less than the value of the sum of its parts.

It follows that use rights must be part of the original bundle of property rights granted to the first occupant. Yet just what do these "use rights" consist of? The vulgar conception is to claim that the right to use property permits one individual to use his gun to kill his neighbor or use his land to pollute his neighbor. No legal system, to my knowledge, has ever adopted so odd, expansive, and indefensible a position.[1] A property owner must have *exclusive* use of his property, but it hardly follows that he should have *unlimited* use of that property. In all cases, the key challenge for the legal system is to identify the set of consistent property uses that maximizes the value of the holdings of all individuals within the group, taking into account all interactive effects, positive and negative, between neighbors.

The first constraint in setting system-wide rules is one of equal entitlements for all landowners. Any effort to create legal preferences for one person or another must decide who gets what advantages and why. The departure from formal equality thus creates a complex strategic game that no one can win, precisely because everyone can play. In contrast, formal equality creates a focal point of equilibrium that is easily observed and honored, and thus puts an effective damper on the factional intrigue that threatens to bring down the entire system. So the first working assumption is that a sound system of land use regulation should protect the *like* liberty of all owners to use their property as they please. From our earlier discussion, we know that all such uses will take place only if they provide benefits for their owners, and if each benefit counts as a presumptive social improvement.

Use rights, then, are part of the bundle. But *which* uses are entitled to legal protection and which are not? Stated otherwise, what limitations on land use are likely to increase the value of all parcels of land when universally and reciprocally applied? Historically, both civil-law and common-law systems started the ball rolling by tying liability to physical *entry* and *invasions*. Sending bullets onto the land of others counts as a trespass to land; sending fumes, noise, and dust counts as a common-law nuisance. Finding the exact boundary line between trespass and nuisance takes a good deal of ingenuity in borderline cases, such as when waste stored on one parcel of land leaks onto another.[2] Those details of classification may influence the choice of sub-rules (such as the statute of limitations) in different cases, but they don't play a critical role in fleshing out the basic structure of the system. The general view, empirically based, is that the gains from trespasses and nuisances to the owner who brings them about are presumptively smaller than the losses inflicted on the neighbor. Clear boundary lines reduce enforcement costs on the one hand, and help to preserve the stability of ownership rights on the other.

The key to making this system work is to confine the generalized notion of harm to some physical predicate, so that the Millian harm exception does not swallow the basic rule. In order to do that, it is necessary to develop a coherent account of the causation of harm—one that respects the distinction between real and pecuniary externalities outlined in Chapter 3. The best way to do this is to start with the easy cases and then work out to the hard ones. That was done, albeit without deep philosophical reflection, in the Roman-law system that tied the infliction of harm—especially the killing of slaves and herd animals—to the direct application of force by one person to another; in the graphic Roman language, this was phrased as *corpore corpori*, or "by the body to the body."[3] The early English equivalent of this notion is the direct application of force by one person to another. There are obvious debates about whether the use of instruments to inflict harm changes the legal relationship between the parties, to which the answer was always no. If you cannot strangle a person with your bare hands, you cannot do it with a rope either. The more delicate philosophical cases arose when the element of directness was missing.

Historically, the two most famous cases of indirect harm were these. A sets poison before B. The harm is indirect because B eats it in ignorance of its deadly qualities. C digs a hole in the road, which is covered with leaves. The harm is indirect when D drives into it, again in ignorance of the lurking danger. In both cases, the same solution applied. So long as a defendant coerces or misleads the victim into eating the food, the chain of causation is not broken. So long the victim was ignorant of the hole in the road or forced to go into it, the chain of causation likewise was not broken. In both cases, actions done under either coercion or deception from the defendant did not sever the connection. The defendant has, in fact, caused the victim's death or injury.

The overall analysis, as indicated earlier, can be extended to cover three or more individuals, so long as the system of pairwise comparisons, outlined in Chapter 3, is observed. Thus, if A digs a hole into which B pushes C, the hierarchy should allow C to recover against either A or B. Once C is out of the picture, the hierarchy of rights between A and B could easily depend on the location of the hole and the intention of the two parties. If A digs the hole on a public right-of-way, only to conceal it with leaves, then B will be able to recover from A, so long as he did not have knowledge of the dangerous condition. But if A digs the hole by mistake, and B pushes C into it on purpose, then the priorities are reversed.

The point of this exercise is to establish clear limits on how far the notion of causation can run. Modernists do not follow this incremental approach but instead ask grander, but less informative, philosophical questions, such as: Was the defendant's action a necessary condition for the harm? Was it a substantial factor in bringing the harm about? Was the harm foreseeable at the time the action took place? Or, was it a so-called "but for" cause (but for the wrongful act of the defendant, the harm would not have occurred)?[4]

Unfortunately, these formulations often obscure the outcomes in individual cases. Sometimes the want of foresight of particular harms wrongly excuses individuals for the direct infliction of harm, as in the case of a person who is struck by a cricket ball from a nearby cricket ground when there was only an infinitesimal probability of its occurrence at the time the ball was struck.[5] In other cases, aggressive application of the foresight test imposes responsibility on one individual for the foolish actions of another. The maker of a machine tool has perfect foresight that some downstream users (those who are at the end of the distribution chain) will alter the equipment or disregard obvious safety precautions. Yet, as discussed previously, it hardly follows from this fact that manufacturers are under a duty to take care to prevent foreseeable misuses and dangerous alterations once their equipment is in the hands of downstream users.[6] The older and more sensible "open and obvious" rule led to more efficient coordination between upstream and downstream users. Instead of having to guard against the foolishness of others, the manufacturer was said to have "the right to expect" that others would play by the rules of the game once the product was in their hands.[7] The open nature of the condition gave downstream users the option to avoid using the machine or to take adequate precautions. Yet downstream users were always protected against traps of which they had no knowledge. In effect, the older rule allowed for an efficient coordination of sequential behavior.

The difficulties with notions of causation and foresight should give us pause in dealing again with the Millian harm principle. When stated in its general form, the principle limits the use of state power to "prevent harm to others."[8] Unfortunately, this general formulation does not begin to explain what kinds of harm are covered and which fall outside its purview. More concretely, Mill's harm principle fails to address the role of *damnum absque iniuria*—harm without legal injury—introduced in Chapter 3. For example, does one cause harm by blocking the view of another over his land? Under the Millian principle, it takes a lot of work on the unarticulated sub-rules to get to the right answer. But starting with the more focused Roman approach, the answer is far clearer. In line with the physical-invasion test, the Roman-law rule has legs: no private-law system has ever accepted the idea that one person cannot build on his land solely because it will block the views of another, and rightly so. Applied universally, treating blocked views on a par with physical invasions leads systematically to lose/lose outcomes, which don't get any better as more and more property owners are made subject to this oppressive legal regime. Under that rule, one person would be unable to build even when the neighbor's lot lay vacant, lest he improperly block his neighbor's future right to build. In equilibrium, both plots remain undeveloped, which minimizes their joint value in the name of preserving interpersonal parity. Expanding the analysis from two parties to many leads to a complete prohibition on real estate development, for it is far more difficult for a large number of people to contract out of a lose/lose situation than a small number.

It is equally dangerous, moreover, to adopt some version of the harm principle that breaks the tie by saying that the first to build has the right to protect views over the land of a neighbor. Applied in this context, the principle leads to a wasteful rush to initial construction that gives the winner control over all land that he surveys. The gains to the one successful party are not likely to exceed the losses sustained by all others. Letting individuals develop in due time, without fear of the loss of rights, creates a parity among neighbors that maximizes the combined value of all holdings in the ex ante state of the world. Better two houses with imperfect views than no development at all. And the principle easily generalizes to multiple parties. The original rule that uses a single action—occupation—to give ownership of the full bundle of rights thus avoids nasty tactical struggles.

But in some cases, of course, that initial empirical guess about the primacy of the physical invasions sets the wrong balance between the neighbors. How ought these errors be corrected? Once again, the use of forced exchanges to create social improvements allows for system-wide corrections in both directions, first by knocking out liability for some physical invasions, and, second, by imposing liability for some noninvasions. The traditional physical-invasion test sets the baseline against which to judge whether further changes count as social improvements. In some cases, the physical-invasion test tends to be relatively rigid, as in cases of actual entry onto the land of another. With these trespasses, there is little reason to adjust the underlying rules to take into account some persistent level of low-level *background* risks. It is usually possible just to keep off the property. That is easy with construction or mining activities, given that standard real surveys can usually establish property boundaries known to all through publication. Cases of actual entry can also be easily controlled, so apart from a few cases of individual necessity—such as the need to escape from violent attackers or major storms—the rules prohibiting unauthorized entry are rigid.

Nuisances vary by frequency, intensity, and extension. Accordingly, this branch of the law requires a more flexible approach, in part because an infinite variety of low-level invasive harms are a common feature of everyday life and are dangerous to stamp out. Ordinary noise, routine smells, and occasional vibration are not easily confined within small plots of land. The same level of pristine separation is thus not possible with the ubiquitous noxious activities that define the law of nuisance. It therefore makes no sense to grant legal remedies against the high volume of low-level interferences. These tend to cancel out, so that all persons are better off with a conscious redefinition of the baseline that avoids constant litigation over trivial wrongs.

To avoid this risk of persistent turmoil between neighbors, all legal systems intuitively gravitate toward a principle of live-and-let-live for reciprocal, low-level harms. One common formulation of the rule is that each party has to bear reasonable risks imposed by others. But in fact, the application of this principle is much more bounded than is commonly appreciated, because it does not require any open-ended inquiry to the costs and benefits of all individual interactions. Under that live-and-let-live principle, everyone is free to engage in activities where the nuisance levels fall below some socially defined reciprocal risk, which will in general (under the so-called "locality rule") tolerate higher levels of interference in crowded industrial areas than in the quiet country-side. The easiest way to understand how this principle is constrained in its application is to take a leaf from the constitutional law of takings: assume that the compensation for each low-level invasion that one suf-fers comes from the ability to inflict a similar low-level invasion on oth-ers. This controlled deviation from hard-edged boundaries works for the benefit of all concerned in both the long and the short run, whether we have two parties or twenty in the mix. So the principle is defended not as a celebration of a system of strict property separation, but as a Pareto improvement over that rigid line, which leaves all parties better off than before in roughly equal amounts. In addition, it satisfies the more stringent test of social welfare—pro rata gains to all affected indi-viduals—precisely because there are no ad hoc interventions that any landowner can make in order to grab a larger share of the social surplus created under the rule (see Chapter 4 above).

Noninvasive actions are amenable to the same analysis. On this point, Justice Oliver Wendell Holmes articulated the basic rule with his usual bluntness: "At common law, a man has a right to build a fence on his own land as high as he pleases, however much it may obstruct his neighbor's light and air."[9] And in general, this rule does not depend on the intent or mental state of the defendant, but is judged "by external standards only."

This modification of the boundary rules is intended to narrow the gap between the initial rigid boundary lines of a naïve property system and the large social objective of improving the operation of the system as a whole, for the long-term benefit of all. Put otherwise, these emen-dations, if properly limited and conceived, satisfy the most rigid test of a social improvement: they improve the lot of all parties in roughly equal proportions. Toward that end, it is also useful to single out classes of activities that are done wholly within boundary lines that generate few gains to the owners but inflict much harm on their neighbors; these are best handled by the same test of reciprocal benefit that lies behind the live-and-let-live rule for invasive nuisances. The most common illustration involves the rules on lateral support: preventing a landowner from removing his land where it supports the vacant land of his neighbors. Stopping the tumbling is more valuable than the right of excavation, within limits. More concretely, that basic obligation cannot be increased by a strategic decision of one landowner to build early on his land in the hope of increasing the support obligation thereby incumbent on his neighbors. The legal countermeasure against this ploy requires the party who wants to dig on his own land only to give advance *notice* to neighbors, who then have time to secure the foundations of their own improvements before the construction begins next door.[10] Beyond that, the right to build is not lost or compromised by the unilateral action of some other landowner. Anyone who sees the possibility that his neighbor will eventually build will back off from construction close to the boundary line, unless he secures some covenant running with the land that protects the broader support right.

There is a second class of noninvasive nuisances that involve blocking views over the land of another. Normally these are nonactionable harms. But there is a narrow class of cases involving "spite fences," for which the general view has been that no one person can erect a fence whose *sole purpose* is to block the view of another. This category of cases is limited in scope because most fences have the additional purpose of securing privacy for their owners. And in any event, the rule does not extend beyond fences to "spite houses," given their high cost of construction and their obvious uses to their owners. The key point here is that the role of malice in settling land use disputes is sufficiently minor that it does not swallow up the basic rule that the blocking of a neighbor's views is not an actionable wrong. In some situations, the rule on spite fences is further stabilized by statutes that immunize all fences under six feet, as well as fences above that height unless the sole or predominant motive is to create harm to neighbors.[11] Once again, these rules are scalable, so that they work as well with many neighbors as with one. These adjustments, taken together, go a long way toward developing a robust set of rules that maximize the joint value of all land subject to the legal regime in a wide range of physical configurations.

Arriving at these solutions, moreover, did not occur by happenstance. Here is one instance in which high theory informed operational rules. The key statement comes from the English jurist Baron Bramwell, who in writing about nuisances as early as 1862, recognized the difference between high-level and low-level interferences and added an additional refinement that attacked nuisances actuated by malice, to which he gave the correct definition: actions from which the only gain to the actor were the harms suffered by other individuals. He saw no reason to allow the live-and-let-live approach to nuisance liability to extend to these cases. Nor was this astute synthesis an accident, for it rested on the fully articulated test of social welfare prior to its articulation in modern economic thought.[12] And why? Because Bramwell recognized that the notion of public interest did not refer to the interest of some disembodied entity. Rather, he was responsive to the aggregation problem that plagues naïve forms of utilitarianism insofar as they treat the public as an undifferentiated mass with a will and interest of its own. Bramwell's view rejected this expansive view by an appeal to methodological individualism, which in turn led him to adopt some imprecise cross between the Pareto and Kaldor-Hicks models of efficiency: "The public consists of all the individuals of it, and a thing is only for the public benefit when it is productive of the good to those individuals on the balance of loss and gain to all. So that if all the loss and gain were borne and received by one individual, he on the whole would be the gainer."[13]

These examples show how the common law develops corrections to the initial no-invasion rule that bring it closer to maximizing some notion of social welfare. The techniques that are used, moreover, do not depend on high levels of judicial discretion. The emphasis is always on objective tests that are easily observable, and thus generate minimum levels of favoritism or expense. Even the malice rules are tightly cordoned off, so that mixed-motive cases are infrequent, and for most critical decisions the hard and clear boundary rules dominate the analysis. The enforcement of these rules, therefore, places little strain on any of the rule-of-law concepts. The rules in question are recognized at common law, so there is no risk of retroactive application. And the statutory exceptions are kept narrow, to avoid the pitfalls of retroactive or targeted legislation.

The process of inclusion and exclusion through incremental modifications, however, suffers from the one limitation that always attaches to general rules. It cannot take into account situations that deviate in some material way from the basic norm. For these situations, the clear delineation of common-law rules has, however, a second virtue: it reduces the transaction costs that have to be incurred to fashion specific contract solutions to correct errors in allocation under the existing property rule. Thus, if one idiosyncratic landowner values the views over the land of another highly enough to *purchase* his neighbor's development rights, a voluntary transfer of rights could leave both sides better off than before. Under the current law of covenants, these agreements in question can be structured to allow the benefits and burdens to extend beyond the original parties—that is, to "run" with the land. Land usually has permanent characteristics, so that what is a beneficial adjustment between the initial parties is likely to work as well for all successors, whether by purchase, gift, or inheritance, on both sides of the transaction. Unlike the rough-and-ready common-law modification to boundary rules between neighbors, these private covenants can be tailored to adopt complex intermediate solutions if desired. For example, a covenant can specify that the owner of the servient tenement (i.e., the party on the bound land) can build to a certain height, and no higher. Those neighbors who are not caught by the covenant remain free to behave as before.

Putting these voluntary land use restrictions into play thus allows any set of two or more neighbors to flip over any legal rule to the extent that this reversal works to the parties' mutual advantage. That adjustment can be made, if need be, with side payments. In practice, it is relatively rare to have one person buy an easement to enter the land of another or to create an actionable nuisance over it. But it is an everyday occurrence for a common owner of a large tract of land to divide it into smaller parcels whose *combined* market value is increased if, pursuant to a common plan, each of these parcels is encumbered with a set of easements (which allow entry over the land of another) and covenants (which restrict otherwise lawful uses of one's own land). One master agreement binding n persons replaces the large number—which in fact is $n(n-1)$—of two-party agreements. Clearly, the greater the number of parties, the greater the transactional savings from the centralized plan. The relative values of the two (or more) parcels could easily shift by creating a complex and reciprocal web of rights, especially if there is some asymmetry in the owners' initial positions. That difference could arise, for example, when one owner (and his successor in title) on the lower portion of the hill takes land subject to height restrictions for new construction for the benefit of the second owner (and his successor in title). But asymmetry of initial positions under a common plan does not create any unfairness or uncompensated externalities among the newly created neighbors. It only leads to an adjustment of the purchase price for the various parcels, so that the price accurately reflects the net benefit or burden from the attached servitudes (lumping together both easements and covenants). So long as the increase in total revenues derived by the single owner exceeds his total costs of creating this more complicated rights structure, a complex system generates a Pareto improvement, which enhances overall welfare. The system is also supportive of rule-of-law considerations, as it limits judicial discretion. Courts are asked neither to draft the covenants nor to speculate about their worth to the parties. They are simply asked to interpret them consistently with the expressed intentions of the parties.

Rights and Remedies

The law governing land use does not deal only with the delineation of rights between neighbors. It must also govern the choice of remedies in land use disputes. On this question, it is straightforward to award damages for harms already caused or to enjoin by legal order those which are now taking place. The hardest question, however, deals with *threatened* harm, where once again certitude is unobtainable. At this point, it becomes necessary to respond to two different forms of error that are possible under conditions of uncertainty. The first error is to allow the harm to occur by not halting the underlying harmful activity at some prior stage. The second is to halt an underlying activity that, with the benefit of hindsight, would have caused no harm. Striking the right balance between these two errors is critical.

The traditional property rights approach held back from issuing injunctions until the threat of harm was *imminent,* so that any further delay would be reckless. At that moment, the legal system became unrelenting, so that the activity had to be stopped in its tracks regardless of the cost and inconvenience that it imposed on the wrongdoer. Thereafter, the remedy could be adjusted so that damages could pick up the loss in the event that the injunction was underinclusive.

This approach—be rigid but late—gets the balance exactly right. The late application of the clear, but tough, standard influences all conduct that takes place prior to its possible application. Every land developer who faces a potential threat of tort damages coupled with a possible shutting-down of his facilities will respond *in advance* by altering his or her activities so as to steer clear of the danger zone. The occasions calling for legal remedy will be rare, and the state's role in overseeing land use decisions will be correspondingly small. This approach makes it virtually impossible to commandeer the nuisance law as a tool to shut down the competitive activities of neighbors, and it dispenses with the need for an endless and arbitrary permitting process for virtually all land uses. Accordingly, this approach inhibits the luxuriant growth of the modern administrative state, which, as will become evident, is given large doses of discretion without a clear principle for its application.

Disposition

A. The Presumption in Favor of Free Alienation

We come next to the last element of a coherent system of property rights: the right to dispose of property. Some of these transactions are commercial and others are gratuitous, but both types of transactions have a key place in an overall scheme of property rights that is sensitive to rule-of-law concerns because neither the court nor the legislature has the discretion to decide which of these agreements to enforce and which not. Indeed, the most important protection offered by the legal system is prior to the creation of any individual contract: it is the right to *select* one's trading partners for their wisdom, wealth, integrity, expertise, and the like. Likewise, the most important feature of a successful charity is the ability of donors to choose their intended beneficiaries, whom they can then monitor or assist at relatively low cost. Both types of arrangements generate complex and nuanced ongoing relationships that can never be fully fleshed out simply by imposing the duty of forbearance appropriate in stranger cases. Dense relationships are not well regulated by the few off-the-rack rules that help to keep unrelated persons apart. Moreover, this presumption in favor of free alienation—the ability to sell to whomever you please—does not apply only to outright transfers. It also covers all situations where the transferor and transferee wish to split either control of the asset or the gains from its use or further disposition. Alienation leads to the creation of complex governance structures of the sort that are common in corporations and condominium associations.

Letting these voluntary transactions unfold one step at a time will generally maximize the gain from the social deployment of any set of assets. In order for this regime to go forward, however, it is necessary to guard against both outright state prohibitions on alienation *and* the full range of taxes and regulations that might burden, but not block, the relevant transactions. The basic model is as follows. A successful voluntary transaction will typically generate a joint gain equal to the sum of the consumer and producer surplus, which the parties divide between themselves. The imposition of any tax that exceeds in dollars the size of the joint gain will abort the transaction, by making it unprofitable. Keeping those levies low, and using them only when they generate return benefits to the parties to offset the taxes, becomes critical. Once again, in the absence of any magical way to measure the gains from voluntary transactions, it is best to follow the Coasean insight by minimizing transaction costs.

B. Justifications on Restraints

With respect to the full range of voluntary dispositions, the next question is whether all government restraints on the ability to dispose of property should necessarily be regarded as per se improper. The answer is no. In some instances, restraints on alienation can be justified along lines that parallel the justifications of the use rights attached to private property. In general, the presumption in favor of the freedom of disposition survives unless or until it is upset in one of two ways. The first is imbalance between the transacting parties, including traditional concerns such as duress, misrepresentation, concealment, mistake, and incapacity. This elaborate body of rules on contract formation is intended to strike at impaired transactions where the background conditions are not conducive to maximizing the joint gains for the parties—the raison d'être for voluntary transactions.

It is critical, however, to make sure that these justifications are not construed so broadly as to undermine the basic system of voluntary exchange and donation. Accordingly, the idea of duress should include not only the threats of force by one person against another, but also cases of "duress of goods," whereby one person threatens not to perform a prior obligation unless he receives additional consideration for his efforts.[14] No contract is stable if its renegotiation can be forced by a deliberate breach of the original or some collateral agreement. Take the simplest case: a contract to clean garments for $10. Once the goods are delivered, the owner should be able to recover the garments by paying the stipulated price to the other contracting party, who cannot be allowed to use this bit of transaction-specific monopoly power to withhold return of the goods until he receives, say, $12. The owner should have the option to sue for the return of the goods on payment of the original contract price, or to pay the excess and sue for its recovery. Otherwise, unilateral variation of terms would undermine the security of exchange in all cases.

By the same token, it would be a huge mistake to unmoor this notion of economic duress from traditional conceptions of property rights. Thus, no one should be allowed to set aside contracts (or to prevent their formation in the first place) because of a marked inequality of wealth between the contracting parties. The common popular conception is that many of these contracts are exploitive. The usual proposal is some prohibition to prevent the weaker party from entering into what, from the outside, looks like a losing transaction. But this argument ignores the simple point that so long as coercion and deception are put to one side, each transactor will only enter a transaction that leaves him better off than before, no matter his initial level of wealth. Poor people have, if anything, a greater incentive to avoid propositions that compound their fragile economic position. Insisting that the right to dispose of property or labor should be limited upon some a priori division of the transactional gains only reduces the options available to both parties, thereby diminishing or eliminating the prospect of gains from trade.

More concretely, Franklin Roosevelt's maxim that "necessitous men are not free"[15] should *never* be applied to cases of general poverty on the ground that it is just a small extension of the rule that has long let courts revise contracts concluded under conditions of physical necessity—i.e., persons in danger of death or serious bodily harm who can deal with only a single person.[16] In those circumstances, the correct response limits the dominant party to a risk-adjusted competitive rate of return on his investment, which must be preserved so as not to eliminate the prospect that certain firms, such as commercial salvors, will stand ready to assist others in times of distress.[17] But general economic disadvantage does not involve that sharp truncation of options. In those cases, the appeal to necessity ignores the radical difference that arises in competitive labor markets where employment choices are widespread—at least if state intervention, done in the name of the "protection" of the poor, does not reduce its scope.

This concern with market structure points to a second sensible limitation on freedom of alienation within a liberal system, which deals, as previously discussed, with contracts to commit ordinary wrongs against third persons, such as murder, theft, or rape. The dangers of external harm, however, are not limited only to settings where two parties *intend* to inflict harm against a third person. A complete set of restraints on alienation must also cover situations where certain voluntary transactions increase the risk that some unintended harm will occur. The sale of a gun to a minor may increase the risk of harms to third parties stemming from its improvident use. The sale of alcohol to teenagers may well have the same tendency.

One possible strategy is to ignore the actions that lead up to the actual harm, instead concentrating all enforcement actions, both civil and criminal, against the immediate perpetrator of the harm. This approach certainly reduces administrative costs, but it is subject to major flaws of its own. First, direct remedies may not prevent death or serious bodily injury, for which perfect compensation after the fact is, in principle, unavailable. Second, the immediate perpetrators may not be financially capable of answering for their wrongs, thereby undermining the deterrent effect of the damage remedy. In these cases, the ability to restrict the contractual freedom of the immediate wrongdoer opens a new set of useful control possibilities. This has the downside of blocking gainful arrangements that generate no third-party harms. Many people who buy drinks in bars after 2:00 A.M. do not drive, or do not drive danger-ously. But even though that is indubitably true, the converse proposi-tion looms larger. Enough drunk drivers will kill precisely because they have access to alcohol after 2:00 A.M. to justify regulating those sales. The social task is to try to get a sense of clear administrative rules that minimize the sum of the two types of errors. But this could easily involve prohibitions against certain types of voluntary behaviors that may turn out to be harmless, so balance is critical. What applies to a sale of liquor in the early morning need not apply to the sale of beer in su-permarkets during ordinary business hours. As a general matter, mis-takes of over- and underinclusion are likely to be made. But so long as legislators work within the proper remedial framework, they should be able to avoid lurching prematurely to either extreme.

Overview

At this point, the argument has gone through four stages. The first stage identifies the positive features of the rule of law. The second explains the role for both administrative discretion and notions of reasonableness, within the larger framework. The third stage outlines the system of property rights, both private and public, that offers the best path for the realization of the greatest value from human and social resources. The fourth stage recognizes that the set of substantive rights so created is consistent with each and every requirement of the rule of law, as articu-lated on grounds that are no way linked, expressly or by implication, to the system of property rights in question. Nonetheless, the fit is very tight. The system of property rights clearly allocates all rights over all things, and offers means, by contract, gift, or otherwise, to change the initial distribution when appropriate. The clarity of the rights, the abil-ity to know of them in advance, their stability over time, and their rela-tive simplicity all combine to restrict the levels of political discretion that are always a threat to the long-term soundness of any legal system. The same is not true of the complex set of legislative commands that come out of the modern administrative state. Logically, these may be consistent with the rule of law. Practically, as we shall see, they are not.

One way in which to test that notion is to look at two different approaches to one critical aspect of government activities: the power of eminent domain, broadly conceived.

7

Eminent Domain

Why Necessary

This analysis of property rights and the rule of law has thus far established how substance and procedure work together toward a common end. In order to further the analysis, however, we must explain how the conscious use of coercive state power, so critical in the creation of roads and other forms of social infrastructure, can be exercised in a fashion consistent with the rule of law. The need for the use of state power arises, of course, in many recurrent contexts, in which voluntary efforts are likely to fail. The key variable here is often a simple matter of numbers, which operate in different ways in different contexts. When a given person needs the cooperation of only one seller in a given market, the larger the number of participants, the greater the choices, and the less the need for any government intervention. But when the cooperation of all individuals is necessary to achieve a given end, the increase in numbers is likely to lead to systemic bargaining breakdown, which some form of state intervention might alleviate. The exact turning point is often quite low—in some contexts, as few as five or six people will find it impossible to reach agreement on the management of a common resource, such as an underground oil and gas field that extends under their separate surface holdings. Many critical ventures require the cooperation of many more parties. Thus, any effort to purchase lands for a highway in a voluntary market with thousands of separate owners will end in political impasse. A single holdout can disrupt any network. A dozen or a thousand holdouts are certain to do so.

The high transaction costs of real estate assembly explain why the government frequently resorts to a common mode of state coercion—eminent domain—notwithstanding the risk that this historic use of state power poses to the rule of law. The phrase "eminent domain" suggests the dominance of public ownership over private right. Eminent domain empowers the state to forcibly displace private owners from their property for public use, so long as the state compensates them for their lost value—no easy calculation—when it takes that property. At this point, the central inquiry is how to discipline this "takings power" so that it does not run roughshod over the institution of private property that it is designed to buttress. The roadmap for this inquiry is found in the Takings Clause of the Fifth Amendment: "nor shall private property be taken for public use without just compensation."[1]

Right at the outset, it should be apparent that these words only place a limitation on the exercise of government discretion. Nothing in the words of the Takings Clause indicates how government officials should decide which lands ought to be taken for what projects. Those are, in the end, political and social judgments that no abstract constitutional principle can answer. What a constitution can do, however, is constrain the exercise of that government discretion so that it is more likely to lead to the exercise of public force on behalf of public, not partisan, ends. Indeed, one way to think of this analysis of the Takings Clause is as a guide to sound public administration. To get to that result, however, requires a careful integration of the four key components to the inquiry. The first of these asks what it means to take private property. The second asks when that taking is for a public use. The third asks whether just compensation has been provided. The fourth asks how the state, by use of its police power, can justify its takings.

Takings

The initial question concerns the scope of the basic prohibition against the taking of private property that the U.S. Constitution, and other constitutions, impose on all exercises of government power. Everyone agrees, as they must, that the protection of private property is empty if it does not require the state to compensate for the permanent occupation of a private plot of land.[2] No system of property rights rests on the premise that the state may bestow or deny rights in things to private persons on whatever terms it sees fit. Rather, the correct starting point is the Lockean position that property rights come from the bottom up. In the state of nature, all particular things are unowned. Thereafter, the first possessor acquires by a unilateral act rights that are good against the rest of the world. The state fulfills its role of protecting these property rights against encroachment by creating a "social contract," whereby individuals are required to surrender some portion of what they own so as to provide for the greater security of that which they retain.

The definitions of "private property" that animate the private law must necessarily cover the public law as well. All other approaches run the risk of dangerous political arbitrage between private disputes and public administration. Normally, individuals must secure easements to enter land belonging to others or covenants to restrict how others may use their land beyond the limitations implicit in the law of nuisance. If those understandings, however, applied only to disputes between private individuals, and not to government actions, one simple strategy could topple the entire edifice of property rights. Potential buyers of covenants and easements would resort to the political process to achieve their objectives, without securing the consent of the individuals over whose property these easements and covenants are taken. If this strategy is allowed in one case, it will be practiced in all. If, for example, one landowner refused to limit the height of his beachfront house to allow two others to view the beach, a local government consisting solely of these three persons could vote two-to-one to impose, without compensation, height restrictions applicable only to beachfront property. The same risk remains in more complex settings involving greater numbers of people, whenever persuading legislators to vote their way is cheaper than paying off an owner for his property loss.

Substituting politics for voluntary transactions has two negative effects. First, it wastes resources on politicking rather than spending them on productive activities. Second, it allows the political majority to prevail without offering any assurance that the gains it secures are larger than the losses inflicted on its adversaries. Official public action thus remains stubbornly opaque as to whether the government action makes matters better or worse overall. The response to this sorry state of affairs relies on the same "agency" approach used in dealing with permits and injunctions. Under that approach, the state, in using its eminent-domain power, has only the same rights vis-à-vis its citizens that those citizens themselves have. State action is used to overcome the transaction cost barriers to coordinating sensible collective action, much the way civil class actions aggregate the small interests of many parties. Eminent domain is not an "open sesame" that allows those parties to obtain greater rights through politics than they could have acquired by banding together to assert their claims against their neighbors when the costs of forming their coalition are zero.

At this point we must ask what cases—apart from outright permanent dispossessions—are covered by the Takings Clause. Government actors (such as private taxpayers anxious to avoid taxation of ordinary income) will resort to ingenious schemes to circumvent constitutional restraints on their power. It is therefore necessary to ensure that the takings prohibition (like analogous constitutional protections of freedom of speech and religion) covers not only outright permanent dispossession, but also a set of substitute strategies that governments—or, more accurately, the dominant factions that control them—could otherwise adopt to circumvent the applicable constitutional constraints. The proper technique for sorting out the various scenarios depends on the key common-law distinction between actions that reduce property value through direct competition and those that reduce property value by removing the various incidents—exclusive possession, use, and disposition—of the property for the benefit of others. The legal system cannot be viable if different tests of the compensability of these actions are used in the public and private domains.

Thus, the loss in value resulting from state action should be compensated in the same fashion, no matter whether the land is occupied or its use is restricted. In all cases, the overall maxim must be that "the more you take, the more you pay." Otherwise, the political temptations are irresistible to engage in excessive regulation. Let the occupation of the land cost the government $100 when its value to the state is only $90, and the odds are good that the government will not condemn unless its own political processes are sadly awry. But if land use regulation benefits the government $40 when it costs the owner $80, the state will not regulate if compensation is required, but may well regulate if it is not. The political risks of factional dominance and state misbehavior are the same whether we speak of regulation or occupation. The decision to use a light-handed approach to land use restrictions thus drives modern law off the rails in two ways. First, it abandons the per se rule of compensation for certain types of occupations. Second, it does not afford full compensation for "mere restrictions" on land use, but instead adopts a test that awards nothing for uses lost so long as uses retained have some residual value. To see how this analysis plays out, it is critical to examine the fate under modern law of the three key incidents of property law: possession, use, and disposition.

DISPOSSESSION. The paradigmatic case of a taking arises when the government orders someone off his land today, whether it occupies the land itself or permits some private person to enter. But the scope of the principle is not limited to those cases. The same per se rule would apply even if the state were willing to wait for a period of years before entering into occupation of, say, public parks in twenty years or after the death of the current occupant. Nonetheless, the law succumbs to the willingness to treat a dispossession ordered tomorrow differently from one ordered today. Rent control illustrates the basic problem. Under traditional property conceptions, a tenant must vacate at the end of the lease to respect the temporal dimension of property. Rent control laws allow the tenant to remain in physical possession of the premises after expiration of his or her lease at a below-market rent. Eviction is limited to narrow reasons, such as nonpayment of rent, which simply will not happen when rent is well below market rates. The per se rule of compensation should require that the state make up the difference between market and contract rental either for each monthly period, or in a lump sum, as it chooses. It does neither, because the rent control statutes were first sustained as a temporary wartime measure that in some cases was never repealed.

Older systems of rent control kept rents fixed, even in times of inflation, leading to total economic ruination as landlords could never cover costs. Modern rent stabilization laws treat private landlords like public utilities: they may recover operating expenses, plus a fair return on their invested capital.[3] Typically they cannot be required to accept annual percentage increases below the level of inflation.[4] Unfortunately, this convenient formula assigns all increases in the underlying value of the property to the tenant, and not to the owner. In contrast, all reductions in land values fall on the landlord, as tenants are free to leave unless the landlord lowers the rent. This heads-I-win-tails-you-lose system of accounting should reduce the compensation owing, but not insulate the scheme altogether.[5] And what is true of stabilization statutes is manifestly true of the older rent control statutes that allowed for no increases in rent unless and until a tenant voluntarily vacated the premises.

Under these various rent control schemes, the ever-greater disparity between rental prices and market values inevitably creates major economic dislocations, which generate political pressures in the opposite direction. Often the response is some form of selective vacancy decontrol, especially for high-end units. But these transitions can easily go astray. Thus, the New York Court of Appeals disregarded a long-established administrative reading of the rent stabilization laws to deny rent increases to landlords who had received public subsidies for capital improvements,[6] and the decision threw local markets into immediate turmoil. Rickety rent control schemes can easily spin out of control until the next ad hoc legislative fix generates yet another legal brawl. The system of public administration has to buckle under the strain, because there are no fixed principles to constrain the discretion of just how good a deal sitting tenants should get at the expense of their landlords. The issue is subject to extreme politicization for no social benefit. No wonder the prospect of regulation chills investment in rental properties even in the face of existing housing shortages.

REGULATORY TAKINGS: OF RIGHTS TO USE AND DISPOSITION. Governments are given far more leeway whenever they impose restrictions on land use and disposition, even though the political risks of factional politics are as great as they are in cases of outright dispossession. The current rules recognize that possession, use, and disposition are all sticks in the owner's bundle of rights. The current view then concludes that any bundle of rights is arbitrary, such that the legislature can remove or modify sticks from the bundle more or less at will. This view fails to see how the coherence of the common-law bundle reduces the transaction costs needed to put privately held property into active and profitable use. Arbitrary removal of the incidents of ownership reduces the economic value of these assets.

For this reason, the compensation requirement should also apply to anyone who upsets the various interests in mortgages by insisting by fiat that, for example, a government lien receive priority over an existing mortgage.[7] Moreover, the takings law also applies to state-imposed restraints on alienation, such as those that prevent the leasing or selling of

property to certain individuals. Put otherwise, all the incidents of ownership that are protected against private invalidation or subordination
should receive the same protection against government action. Restricting the law of takings to the simple protection of the right to exclude
has the unfortunate consequence of exposing all elements of use, development, and disposition to state expropriation in ways inconsistent
with the rule of law.

One leading illustration of the risks inherent in this approach is
the Supreme Court's regulatory takings opinion dealing with landmark
preservation programs. *Penn Central Transportation Co. v. City of New
York*[8] arose out of a challenge to New York City's power to deny Penn
Central the right to use its air rights for construction over Grand Central Station, a designated landmark. These air rights are fully protected
under New York state law. They can be sold, mortgaged, or given away
by deed or by will. The *Penn Central* opinion is notable for how Justice
William Brennan violated every norm of classical liberal theory. He refused to recognize this state-law property interest in air rights. Instead,
he flouted the rule of law by insisting that no per se rule could eliminate
the need for "ad hoc" decisions at the end of a laborious administrative
process. In so doing, he falsely equated restrictions on land use with
losses from economic competition, when sound legal theory, as noted
earlier, treats legal restraints and economic competition as polar oppo-
sites. That result would not be possible if the same dense conception of
ownership that governs private disputes carried over to evaluating all
forms of state action.

The effect of these designation decisions is to open up a large sphere
of influence to political intrigue, as it costs the state nothing to designate properties as landmarks, which can have a devastating impact on
owners. In many cases, these designations are avowedly strategic: make
the current building a landmark so that no new construction will follow
in its wake. The system of designation, moreover, does not require the
landowner to maintain the property, which can easily fall into desue-
tude for want of the funds to support it. Nor is any of this necessary.

Private organizations can and do offer to purchase historically significant exteriors from owners, and usually do so by requiring expenditures
for upkeep and maintenance. Tax subsidies could be used to provide an
offset against costs when the exterior is maintained for public benefit.
The use of the Takings Clause does not, of course, answer the question
of which properties should be designated landmarks and which should
not. But by putting a price tag on the exercise of government discretion,
it channels it into more productive directions.

TAKINGS FROM THE MANY AND GIVINGS TO . . . ? Thus far I
have addressed only cases where one person is singled out for special
treatment from the government—cases in which it easy to discern who
bears the burden. But the logic of the Takings Clause also extends to
countless variations on the basic theme. Land held in joint tenancy by a
husband and wife is not deprived of takings protection solely because it
has two owners instead of one. Theoretically, no magic line runs between takings from a few people, which are compensable, and takings
from many individuals, which are commonly treated as noncompens-
able. The present strategy concedes that any occupation of land counts
as a taking, no matter how trivial. But it holds that "mere" restrictions
on the ability of a party to use land or to dispose of it are not compensable, unless for some unexplained reason they go "too far." The general
rule, at least, is that while "property may be regulated to a certain extent, if regulation goes too far it will be recognized as a taking."[9] But
picking some arbitrary point on the continuum of property rights leads
to arbitrary distinctions never tolerated in the private law. Conceptually,
there is no viable breakpoint between "mere" regulations of the use of
real property that do not call for compensation and substantial regulations that do. A single theory has to guide all cases.

Unfortunately, this sound approach has been uniformly rejected
not only in the Supreme Court, but also in most state court decisions.
Notwithstanding the ordinary meaning of the term, judges will not use
the inclusive term "private property" to cover all incidents of ownership

equally. The correct approach spurns these distinctions by following this principle: whatever state limitations on possession, use, and disposition count as a taking from one person—and all do—they *necessarily* count as multiple takings when directed toward many persons. Hence, there is no categorical distinction between a landmark designation statute that targets one house or a small district, and a general zoning ordinance. Land use restrictions count as imposing covenants covered by the Takings Clause. Seizure of land for nonpayment of taxes also counts as a taking, unless the government can defend the validity of the basic tax. Under classical liberal theory, all government actions should be examined under a presumption of error. That presumption is in turn rebuttable, but for reasons far more principled than are commonly understood.

Justifications

The basic sphere of private property is huge, and so, too, is the scope of any constitutional provision that protects it. But the scope of that initial protection should caution against any claim that property rights are absolute. In both public and private contexts, it is necessary to differentiate between those regulations, taxes, and changes in liability rules that produce social improvements and those that do not. That requisite analysis cannot be performed by narrowing linguistically the term "taking" to exclude all regulations, taxation, and liability rule modifications. Rather, as with the law of nuisance, the correct methodology relies on incremental corrections to define the proper scope of government obligations. These corrections require an understanding of the proper principles for dealing with just compensation, public use, and police power.

Just Compensation

Let's begin with just compensation. State coercion should be used to overcome the barriers of high transaction costs by seeking, to the extent institutionally feasible, to leave those persons subjected to the state's coercive power *at least as well off* after its imposition as they were before. In some cases, this test cashes out quite simply. Let the state take an isolated parcel of land, and it must pay the owner the sum of money needed to restore him to the level of wealth he enjoyed in the pre-taking state of affairs. Once that is done, the individual may also be in a position to share the gains from the social project, which leaves him *better off* to the same degree as his fellow citizens. This project will get off the ground only if the state is required to use the correct measure of compensation, one that covers not only the fair market value of the condemned property, but also its full subjective value—which exceeds market value for the vast majority of people who have not posted "For Sale" signs on their front lawns or factory gates. In addition, just paying for the "property taken" does not achieve the proper social goal. In particular, the state should compensate for the "consequential" losses associated with forced dispossession, including legal and appraisal fees, loss of good will tied to businesses at particular locations, moving and relocation expenses, and any taxable gain triggered by the forced sale of appreciated property.[10] Generally, however, these losses are ignored, for the odd reason that they are not also gains to the government.[11]

On the other side of the ledger, the government should receive a *credit* against any compensation it owes for any *enhancement* of value to any retained property. Sometimes these offsets are negligible, but on other occasions they could prove quite dramatic. Constructing a government highway or railroad in some isolated region may often require *no* compensation for the land taken. The increased value of the *retained* land (e.g., from easy highway access) could well exceed the value of the lost property. These offsets indicate that any full economic accounting must include the *implicit-in-kind* compensation associated with any real property. What a property owner receives from government action belongs in the mix as an offset to the property that has been taken away.

Oftentimes, *no* cash compensation is required with comprehensive taxation or regulation, if the overall program returns benefits in excess of the respective burdens on the individuals who are regulated or taxed. Out of this argument comes, I think, a strong case for the now-unfashionable flat tax, which has appealed to classical liberal thinkers ranging from Adam Smith to Friedrich Hayek.[12] A flat-tax system allows the government to determine its own revenue requirements, free of all ad hoc maximum restraints on revenue that could prove inconvenient, or worse, in times of war or acute national distress. The flat-tax position therefore escapes the charge, frequently lodged against strong libertarians, of treating all taxation as theft while ignoring its return benefits to the parties taxed. The key objective of this flat-tax regime is to closely approximate the most demanding standard of social welfare by helping to match, for each person in the polity, his fraction of the social costs to his fraction of the social benefits. This one test places a persistent financial check on the willingness of dominant social factions to overtax a small fraction of the overall population for partisan gains. (Today the United States collects more in income tax from the top 1 percent of earners than from the bottom 95 percent of taxpayers. Ouch.) A taxation regime that systematically insulates any fraction of the population, however poor, from the burdens shared by the rest of society creates a modern *rentier* class that lives off of expanding government programs, to which they are asked contribute nothing. Thus, "refundable tax credits" for those who pay no taxes have a deleterious effect on political deliberation by inducing people to vote for those political figures who promise them, in effect, free benefits.

Taxation and regulation, then, should be limited to those collective goals that cannot be obtained through voluntary arrangements, such as preservation of the social order, defense, and infrastructure. The flat tax thus reduces the level of the government's political discretion without limiting its power to meet its revenue needs, large or small. Second, notwithstanding the difficulties of tracing the pattern of benefits from government programs, the flat tax rests on the simplest working hypothesis, which treats those benefits as proportionate to income. Indeed, this flat tax systematically favors those individuals located at the *bottom* of the income distribution, because everyone, rich or poor, attaches a large value to bodily integrity and personal security. Low-income individuals are taxed only on their tangible assets, which constitute a smaller portion of their total endowments than is the case for richer persons. Using this device thus encourages people to expand their own wealth, which in turn should limit the percentage of total private wealth taken through taxation, thereby further spurring productive activities. The implicit emphasis on growth is, moreover, not misplaced. During the course of a single year, a 2 percent increase in gross domestic product (GDP) does not sound like it is much less than a 3 percent increase in GDP. But the difference becomes manifest through the miracle of compound interest, which works out to a difference in growth rates of about 22–34 percent in ten years and 624–1,820 percent over a century. The price of antigrowth policies is steep, which is all too evident in a country that has been mired in a virtual recession for the past several years, and whose devotion to a short-term principle of supposed equity carries with it a very high price tag.

Public Use

The constitutional restriction against takings that are not for public use is clearly necessary to prevent a rich and powerful individual from exploiting the eminent-domain power to obtain his neighbor's property without having to meet the owner's price. But how far-reaching is this prohibition against government use of the eminent-domain power? Surely it does not extend to takings for roads, parks, or official buildings—much less those whose doors, like the Pentagon's, are shut to the public at large.

The harder cases arise when transactional obstacles block sensible resource use. For example, in the nineteenth century, mill owners were allowed to flood farmland owned by multiple other persons, in order to create sufficient water pressure to power their mills.[13] High transaction costs were again key in reaching the right result. After all, many small farms had to be flooded in order for the mill to be viable. Thus, the objections of a single well-placed landowner could scuttle the whole project—effectively giving each landowner a "veto" power over the transaction. A similar scenario arises when the owner of scrub-lands wants to block overhead trams needed to transport ore to a nearby railroad or to build irrigation ditches over lands belonging to another.[14] The old Supreme Court nervously extended the public-use doctrine to these cases of private necessity, but only when "absolutely necessary," and only with the exercise of "great caution." In contrast, the modern view ignores these worries of government abuse and allows property to be taken, in the misguided effort to increase the tax base of ordinary towns.

The historical protection of the public-use provision has been eroded in three key Supreme Court cases, designed to expand the ability of government to engage in land planning. The 1954 case of *Berman v. Parker*[15] permitted takings of usable property located in a "blighted" area on solely aesthetic grounds. Next, *Hawaii Housing Authority v. Midkiff*[16] read the public-use requirement as merely the need for "a conceivable public purpose." Virtually every government action can meet this version of the "rational-basis test," which places virtually no viable limits on either economic or retroactive legislation. In *Midkiff*, this formula allowed the tenant to pay money into a government fund to buy the landlord's interest, which was then transferred to the tenant, ostensibly to break up a land "oligarchy." Next, in 2005, the Supreme Court decided *Kelo v. City of New London,*[17] which upheld the condemnation of ordinary homes in order to expand the tax base. New London had, however, no immediate plans to use the land, which was still lying vacant six years after condemnation.

Kelo was met with widespread public outrage,[18] while twenty-one years earlier *Midkiff* had been passed over in silence. The difference in response is best attributed to the ability of ordinary people to identify more closely with dispossessed homeowners than with the fat-cat landlords whose main interest in the land was financial, in the form of a stream of rental payments from their tenants. But the systematic source of social concern is that this new reservoir of government discretion clouds all land titles, a situation that could subsequently discourage private investment in real estate by people fearful that their property might be condemned for a fraction of its value. Worse still, governments often cut back their maintenance of public facilities in areas in which they target properties for condemnation, in order to reduce the value of property they plan to condemn.

Kelo took place after extensive public deliberations—a fact which again provides warning that when property protections are weak, a powerful majority can use deliberation to organize a coalition to run roughshod over some weak minority group. Nonetheless, the deliberation requirement is not entirely toothless, for it offers some modest protection against private parties who may wish to implement a hidden agenda of their own. Yet at the same time, the sad rule of politics is that once the Supreme Court moves the boundary line of permissible government action outward, some astute political group will move to take advantage of the new political opportunities. Just that risk of private takings arose in the Texas condemnation of gates at Dallas Love Field, home of Southwest Airlines.

The 1979 Wright Amendment (Jim Wright, who was then Speaker of the U.S. House of Representatives, hailed from Fort Worth) restricted long-haul flights in and out of Love Field to planes that had no more than fifty-six seats.[19] Wright's specially concocted amendment protected American Airlines' dominant market position at the new Dallas–Fort Worth Airport, which had been funded by revenue bonds that might prove difficult to pay off if the upstart Southwest Airlines could expand its operation at Love Field, located close to downtown Dallas.[20] In a blatant piece of special-interest legislation, the Wright Amendment became the unfortunate coda to the general deregulation of the airlines that had been completed a year before.[21] This ad hoc arrangement was sustained against constitutional challenge under an all-too-pliable rational-basis test, which gave undeserved discretion to political actors—the sort of power that comports badly with any notion of the rule of law.[22]

When that arrangement grew economically untenable twenty-five years later, Southwest Airlines, American Airlines, and the Dallas–Fort Worth Airport, along with the cities of Dallas and Fort Worth, negotiated a plan to repeal the Wright Amendment by 2014 with this catch: blow up key gates at Love Field not owned by Southwest, to prevent future competition by new market entrants. The per se restraint of trade received congressional blessing under the Wright Amendment Reform Act of 2006,[23] on the frivolous ground that only in Dallas did gates have to be destroyed to control pollution or reduce congestion. Once again, specious police-power arguments blessed a manifestly anticompetitive purpose. Yet the terminal owners (with whom I consulted) did not raise a post-*Kelo* takings challenge, out of fear that the argument that lost in the one case might not win in the next.

The feebleness of the post-*Kelo* public-use requirement was equally evident in *Didden v. Village of Port Chester*,[24] where the town vested in a single developer, Greg Wasser, the right to approve or disapprove all new construction in Port Chester. When local landowners Bart Didden and Dominick Bologna proposed to build a new CVS pharmacy on a Port Chester site, Wasser said that he would have the Village condemn the land unless he received either a partial interest in the project or a payment of $800,000. When Didden refused, Wasser was able to have the land condemned shortly thereafter and built his own Walgreen's pharmacy on the site. A Second Circuit panel, which included Sonia Sotomayor (now a Supreme Court justice), upheld the decision. Takings from A to B are alive and well under the United States Constitution.

The dangers of this modern approach should be evident. The supposed gains from allowing the state to manage the overall land use system are more than offset by the insecurity of ownership that deters ordinary people from improving their property, so long as the risk of ruinous condemnation at bargain prices remains. Ironically, this sorry tale of the dispossession of ordinary people from their homes arises in part because pervasive zoning regulation blocks needed real estate development that would otherwise be obtainable through voluntary arrangements. Developers who are blocked by the government thus turn to the government to obtain condemned sites blessed with the needed government permits. By allowing takings for any "conceivable" public use, the modern law thus opens the system up to a level of intrigue wholly inconsistent with the rule of law.

Police Power

The third element in the analysis of the government's takings power relates to the government's police power, which, building on the common law of nuisance, allows the restriction of certain activities *without* any compensation at all. The traditional formulation of the police power—the ability of the state to impose limitations on the liberty and property of those subject to its control in the name of "safety, health, good morals and the general welfare"—has been stretched beyond recognition, especially in its last two components. But the good sense behind the police power requirement rests on the now-familiar need to cope with the problem of high transaction costs.

As noted earlier, the core cases of nuisance involve situations in which one person pollutes the land or water of his neighbor (see Chapter 3). The organization of common-law rules tended to promote global efficiency through the development of the law of nuisance. To the extent that those insights are carried over into the modern law, all is well. To the extent that the conception is expanded beyond its common-law roots, trouble awaits. The initial challenge in this area is that pollution comes in all sizes and shapes. Emissions from millions of tailpipes could pollute the air that millions of people—including those responsible for emitting the pollutants—breathe. Even the staunchest defender of private property has to shy away from the mind-boggling complexity of countless private lawsuits, whether brought as individual or as class action lawsuits. The police power may therefore be invoked, because with pollution it meets this one test: the state may, by administrative action, fine, limit, or ban those activities against which citizens could bring valid private lawsuits to collect damages or obtain injunctions, if only they can afford the expenses of litigation. The state's extensive permit power should be constrained solely to these ends. It does not expand to cover other objectives, such as the suppression of competition, that frustrate the legitimate objectives of classical liberal theory.[25]

This "agency" theory of government is *not* intended to give the state new worlds to conquer through legislation. Its sole function is to pick up the enforcement shortfall of private lawsuits. The definition of "nuisance" remains unchanged, as does the requirement that allows injunctive relief only for actual or imminent harms. The basic objective is to prevent political arbitrage that allows people to gain, through politics, ends that they could not obtain through private litigation. The source of the pollution does not matter; what is important is the amount and toxicity of those emissions. The most sensible approach always attacks the most serious conditions first, and tolerates the same level of low background pollution—no dead silence in large cities—already built into the private law of nuisance.

This classical liberal position must of course make key adjustments for distinctive risks such as nuclear power, where catastrophic failure could occur without warning. Even tort liability backed by substantial insurance cannot compensate the dead or severely injured. Hence, ongoing inspections before the fact are an essential part of the overall regulatory process. These inspections, in turn, must be conducted, or at least organized, by government agencies, because no individual or small group will bear all the costs of a venture that benefits the community at large. The inspections should be focused on safety only. The difficult question is how to balance the two forms of error that always arise under conditions of uncertainty. Do we allow dangerous facilities to operate with lax inspection? Or do we keep safe facilities out of service with overly strict inspections?

The current strategy tends to err on the side of keeping dangerous items out of service. But often this strategy goes overboard and thus increases overall systemic risk by inducing private parties to keep rickety older facilities in service long past their productive peak. No new nuclear power plant has been put in service in the United States since the serious incident at Three Mile Island in 1978. The utter unwillingness to bear some residual risk (which shrinks with technological experience) has exposed the nation to the alternative peril of the emissions from carbon fuels, and tends to keep existing nuclear plants in service even after they have become obsolete. The ability of administrators and judges to insist on impossible safety standards for new projects should thus be stoutly resisted in administrative law.[26] In many risky ventures, such as constructing buildings, roads, and bridges, or the drilling and shipping of oil, overregulation usually counts as the greater peril. When these activities are undertaken by responsible parties, private insurers and inspection societies are usually better-positioned than government officials to monitor these activities. For in these instances, the common-law approach of imposing late but tough restrictions carries over without a hitch. All of these activities should face quick government shut-downs and fines in the event of actual or imminent harm, thereby relaxing the complex permitting process that routinely strangles new projects today.

The present system not only relaxes the imminence requirement, insofar as it deals with means/ends connections; it also vastly expands the class of "legitimate" ends that justify, under an elastic account of the "police power," regulation without compensation. The decline of the antinuisance requirement has had its greatest effect on environmental issues. Filling in wetlands, building on real estate used by wild animals for foraging, and cutting down timber that houses endangered species now become wrongs that states can enjoin without compensation,[27] as all ordinary land use is now treated like a nuisance. At this point, the landowner is relegated to an all-purpose wrongdoer who is now under a duty to "mitigate" the costs of new land uses by offering compensation *to* the government to offset its supposed losses. The roles of aggressor and victim have in effect been reversed.

Applied to urban settings, the broad swath of public powers allows local governments to impose large-lot, setback, and height restrictions on the construction of new homes. In addition, local governments may use zoning restrictions to forbid new construction that some committee deems "incompatible" with the character of the neighborhood. Likewise, the power to designate structures for existing landmark preservation is largely unlimited, and it can result in huge declines in economic value when the "freezing" of a building's exterior complicates both external additions and internal renovations.

A broad set of ends begets complex procedural rules that grant veto power to strategic actors within the system—all in the name of the public interest. Doug Kaplan, a California developer, describes the low-level obstacles as follows. Start by filing a permit application. Sounds easy, at least if you could file online or by mail. It is a lot harder if the application must be submitted by phone to a public official who is never in his office. A routine ministerial act now requires mastery of the fine art of repeat dialing, to beat out other developers who also know the drill. The upshot:

> We submitted 17 sets of plans that were routed to the 14 separate departments, agencies, and individuals who were charged with issuing the dozen separate approvals we needed to build our 2,700-square-foot building. By the time we were finished, we had passed an all-too-familiar milestone in our community: The number of government employees involved in the review and processing of our permits outnumbered the number of construction workers who would eventually build the building.[28]

The complexity in California is matched by the grotesque requirements of the Uniform Land Use Review Process (ULURP), which helps to strangle real estate development in New York City.[29] Its regulatory regimen requires an initial certification, followed by a Community Board Review, a Borough President Review, a City Planning Commission Review, a City Council Review, and a Mayoral Review.[30] Each step brings into play different political coalitions; indeed, negotiating the entire process is akin to threading six needles simultaneously. Laws like ULURP generate spools of red tape that foster the same complex holdout situations that the common-law rules of property rights wisely avoid. Only the owners can build or use—but only if they can overcome the omnipresent array of government vetoes. The same discretion championed in *Midkiff* and *Kelo* increases the degrees of freedom for state regulators.

None of this work was needed to forestall common-law nuisances or put road cuts and service hookups in the right places. And the supposed benefits of public review often do not justify the costs, especially after we add back in the projects lost by landowners who didn't get permits or who decided never to try. Yet the time value of money does not matter when the Supreme Court, resolutely blind to the grim realities of local politics, insists that "normal" (read: "ever-longer") delays do not require compensation for lost use.[31] Matters are made worse by procedural obstacles that bar any judicial challenge until all administrative remedies are "exhausted"—a system that gives local governments strong incentives to add layers to their administrative processes, in order to protect dominant local interests.[32] Getting a federal judge to hear these cases is next to impossible, even to vindicate a federal constitutional right.[33] Nor does the ballot box of local citizens protect nonvoters who would like to move into a community guarded by high permit barriers.

An Integrated System

Any fair appraisal of a regulatory scheme looks at the interplay of all four elements of this synthesis: takings power, just compensation, public use, and police power. This four-part test reflects the commonsense view that the permanent occupation of an isolated plot of land need not be viewed in the same way as a comprehensive zoning ordinance. The Supreme Court case law is therefore correct in subjecting cases of government occupation to a per se rule under which compensation is awarded as a matter of course. The parallel analysis of zoning ordinances does not, however, require a radical leap to the opposite extreme of giving the government carte blanche to impose, without compensation, whatever land use restrictions it chooses, subject only to an elastic rational-basis test that kicks in, if at all, only in the most egregious of circumstances. Instead, the sensible approach begins with a presumption against government power and asks how the three elements of just compensation, public use, and police power work to *expand* the permissible scope of state regulation, while confining it within principled boundaries. To be sure, many zoning ordinances fail because they impose huge losses in value without offering any protection against common-law nuisances that arise—as, for example, when a sandblasting operation is kept out of residential areas. But few cases present these frightening scenarios, because powerful market forces, backed by the ordinary common law of nuisance, usually lead to an effective separation of incompatible land uses.

In some land use contexts, however, a set of cumulative and reciprocal restrictions on all owners within a neighborhood may produce offsetting advantages that augment rather than detract from market value. One illustration is a rule that limits the size and placement of signs on storefronts. Each owner may be required to keep signs flat against the building to enhance the visibility of *all* signs, thereby obviating the need for any cash compensation. Limitations on all building exteriors might preserve the character of a historically significant district. Without regulation, the parties could be caught in a Prisoner's Dilemma in which each modifies his own exterior for short-term gain, thereby destroying the collective good that is obtainable if everyone adheres to the common standard. In complex settings, preservation could produce small losses to owners of historic sites, while generating large gains to the remainder of the community. If so, a well-designed real estate tax abatement scheme on the restricted properties could even out the gains across the entire community, removing the need for additional cash compensation. Rightly used, sound zoning overcomes the serious coordination problems for private owners that voluntary agreements cannot solve.

Taken as a whole, the constitutional inquiry into takings can be restated in nice game-theoretical terms. The use of government power should create win/win situations. Accordingly, a sound takings regime protects *positive-sum* government programs from invalidation, while striking down (given that compensation could never be provided) *negative-sum* projects in which regulation works as a disguised system of wealth transfer. No society can achieve the goal of avoiding negative-sum projects simply by announcing it as some paramount abstract end, unless they also put into play the strong mechanisms needed to control against the evident and persistent risks of factionalism. Given the presumption of government error, the burden should lie on public officials to establish, by a preponderance of the evidence, the soundness of the means used to reach their goals. That task can be achieved only with regulations that provide implicit-in-kind compensation when the standard police power justifications are not available. But this mission cannot be accomplished when zoning laws allow a well-connected citizen to build on the east side of the highway while denying a similar permit to an outsider on the west side. These tests, of course, cannot catch every bad government action. Still, they can eliminate the most obvious abuses of government power, which is all anyone can expect of any institution of social control.

8

Liberty Interests

Classical Synthesis

The same sharp contrast can be drawn between classical liberal and progressive attitudes toward economic liberties. The older model of labor contracts allowed parties to construct their own deals, so that the public force was concentrated on the interpretation and enforcement of their agreements, not on imposing new terms and conditions on all private deals within a given class. In line with that attitude, freedom of contract was the maxim, with respect to both the choice of contracting parties and the choice of contractual terms. There were, of course, exceptions to this rule, but they comported with the modern approach to economic theory that concentrates state interference on markets that cannot achieve a competitive equilibrium. The principle of freedom of contract reaches its zenith in connection with sales and labor contracts that were negotiated in thick markets (that is, with many buyers and sellers), which by definition provide many choices to all persons on both sides of the market. In those markets, the only reason to set aside transactions was the belief that the conditions of their formation would not promote mutual gain through voluntary exchange. So it was that duress, fraud, and infancy, all areas with immense complications, could render a contract unenforceable.

By the same token, however, when markets were no longer thick, the rules changed. For example, common carriers (with either a legal or a de facto monopoly) were subject to obligations to serve all customers on reasonable and nondiscriminatory terms, which had to reflect the best estimate of the costs of service to different customer groups. The rules on contracts in restraint of trade were intended to prevent the monopolization or cartelization of markets. These rules applied across the board to all types of transactions, regardless of the identity of the parties. In general, these prohibitions against horizontal competition—i.e., agreements among buyers or sellers on the same side of the market— work as powerful engines to maximize the social output from scarce resources. The classical liberal tradition in the United States before 1937 was hardly perfect, but on balance it resorted to two major principles to sort out actionable nuisances from competitive harms.

Elements of this synthesis clearly survive today, but the basic attitude of the progressive movement takes a glum view of many voluntary agreements. One common presupposition is that employers (wholly without regard to market structure) have a systematic bargaining advantage over workers. The "inherent" inequality of bargaining power is, to the progressive mindset, a philosophical given that cannot be falsified by any evidence of the improvement of real wages or the reduction of working hours over time. Thus, in the first third of the twentieth century, bitter battles were fought over the constitutionality of wage and hours laws at a time when wages were rising and hours falling as a consequence of the improvement in the overall levels of productivity.

The *Lochner* Challenge

The battle lines of these two worlds came to a head in *Lochner v. New York* (1905),[1] which, by a bare five-to-four majority, struck down a New York criminal statute that set a maximum-hour requirement (sixty hours per week, ten hours per day) for some, but not all, classes of bakers. Consistent with the classical liberal tradition, the *Lochner* court took a dim view of purported health and safety regulations that were intended to stifle competition. The Supreme Court's conclusion was that this regulation was properly classified as a "labor" (unrelated to health and safety) statute that was intended to benefit certain (union) businesses that used two shifts of bakers, working shorter hours. In contrast, Joseph Lochner's business (a bakery in Utica, New York) used only one shift of bakers, whose men slept on the job between preparing the bread at night and getting it ready for shipment in the morning. Nonetheless, the statutory provisions regulating the sanitary conditions in sleeping quarters (which gave an instructive clue as to the source of the long workdays) were not challenged.[2] The hours worked, however, were a bad proxy for exposure, because the nighttime sleeping broke any supposed connection between the length of the workday and exposure to dangerous substances.

The appeal to freedom of contract was not meant to run roughshod over government exercises to protect health and safety. Context matters. Thus, even during the heyday of laissez-faire, seven years before *Lochner*, the Supreme Court upheld maximum-hour legislation in mines and smelters, because the connection between length of workday and health risks in that context is far tighter.[3] More critically, the courts upheld the Federal Employer Liability Act,[4] which eliminated the assumption of risk for dangerous employment on the railroads[5] and abolished the doctrine of common employment (whereby the worker was automatically assumed, in any suit against the employer, to take the risk of negligence by a coworker).[6] In addition, workers' compensation statutes, which displaced the common-law rules of tort for industrial accidents, passed muster, given their close relationship to safety.[7] Finally, a unanimous Supreme Court championed special protective rules for female workers, often on the strength of exhaustive "Brandeis" briefs. These briefs contained only the most perfunctory reference to the applicable constitutional standards, but instead offered, without analysis, an extensive compendium of studies that outlined in the United States and abroad the supposed set of industrial abuses against which maximum-hour laws were intended to guard.[8]

There are two separate grounds on which these health and safety regulations can be challenged. The first approach is to challenge the law as a form of class legislation: Why are some bakers covered and others not? If there is no substantial difference in risk between two competitive types of work, why allow one to be hampered when the other is not? The elaborate classification of bakers in *Lochner* has led to just that suspicion.[9] Yet one consequence of this theory is that the legislature can cure the claimed statutory defect by leveling either up or down. Thus, applying the regulation to cover *both* firms eliminates any supposed inequity even if the two are not in direct competition. But that rule of parity does not prevent the possibility that the broader regulation could be oppressive to both firms, so that both suffer lockstep harms.

The possibility of ratcheting-up state control through comprehensive regulation is, however, eliminated if the statute is attacked on the second ground: that the means chosen have no close connection to a legitimate state end of safety or health. Once that finding is made under a liberty-of-contract theory, the regulation has to be eliminated, no matter how broad or narrow the class of regulated firms. It is no longer possible to cure the defect by extending the regulatory net to other businesses. This liberty-based reasoning resonated more powerfully in the *Lochner* period.[10]

It is important here to stress the modest nature of the judicial intervention. In particular, this traditional legal synthesis allowed the state and federal governments to interfere with employment relations on grounds of health and safety. Yet why should the government tell employers and workers how to interact with each other when their joint conduct poses no risk to third parties? This matter is quite complicated because of the possibility, widely deemed important, that many workplace hazards are beyond the ability of workers to either detect or eliminate. Yet the common-law rules for employer liability (before the rise of the mandatory workers' compensation statutes) drew a set of sensible distinctions to respond to the relevant risks. Liability for latent, or hidden, defects was imposed on firms on the grounds that workers could not be expected to protect themselves against traps. Conversely, liability for obvious defects was restricted only to give the worker an opportunity to protest the condition before leaving, after which the risk was assumed under the wage contract.[11] Note that the early workers' compensation systems that became standard by statute by the end of the First World War had their origins in voluntary plans adopted in two high-risk industries—mines and rails—out of the joint recognition of employers and employees (including unionized workers) that the then-standard tort doctrines that pegged liability to the defendant's negligence, subject to interlocking defenses of contributory negligence and assumption of risk, did not work well in practice.[12]

The historical practice shows the weaknesses of two dominant schools of thought. On the one hand, there are those who insist that all common-law rules of liability gravitate to some efficient norm.[13] That point is incorrect, to the extent that it implies that private agreements in particular businesses could not improve on the public law. The social critics of the common-law regime had a point when they pointed out some of the unavoidable absurdities of the common-law system. Yet it was just those inefficiencies that led to the practice of contracting out. Those disputes, however, would only rarely find their way into the law reports, precisely because industrial-accident cases would normally be resolved through binding arbitration. Indeed, the best evidence of these plans is found in the 1882 case *Griffith v. Earl of Dudley*,[14] which asked whether an early tort reform statute, the Employer Liability Act of 1880, which gave to the employee "the same right of compensation and remedies against the employer as if the workman had not been a workman of nor in the service of the employer, nor engaged in his work."[15] In simpler English, the statute purported to give the workman the same protection against his employer that a stranger would enjoy.

In upholding the right to contract out, *Griffith* did not exhibit a simple waiver by the worker. Rather, it set out the specifics of a comprehensive workmen's compensation program whose detailed institutional design could never have been implemented by any common-law judge, however astute. These elaborate plans falsify the frequent critique that the common law is a relentless exploiter of the laboring man that was so often advanced during the early progressive era.[16] That standard account of worker incompetence does not explain why employers would voluntarily sacrifice a legal defense that they received at common law. It is in the interest of both sides to adopt systems that reduce workplace peril in a cost-effective fashion, at which point the case for state intervention is much weakened. Differential bargaining power has nothing to do with the matter.

Historically, there has never been a time that bona fide health regulation was thought to lie completely outside the police power of the state. But the line between health and safety regulations and anticompetitive regulations held firm in the period between the Civil War and the New Deal, during which time the Supreme Court struck down mandatory collective-bargaining laws at both the federal and the state levels.[17] The court saw no health justification for laws that were intended to displace competitive labor markets with monopolistic unions. In sum, the classical liberal effort to isolate wrongful behavior from competitive behavior was applied in consistent fashion in these contract cases. Once again the articulation of relatively clear principles reduced the level of administrative discretion and thus helped in practice to advance the rule of law.

The Progressive Alternative

The progressive attacks on this system, which eventually proved successful, made a misguided appeal to a notion of necessity that knows no limits. Thus, Roscoe Pound (later dean of Harvard Law School) wrote in his critique of the *Lochner* decision that any appeal to the freedom of contract of "weak and necessitous" bakers "defeats the very end of liberty."[18] All that is lacking is an explanation why this is so, given the tendency of all contracts to work for the mutual gains of both parties. The intellectual unwillingness to confront that objection had, in the end, momentous adverse consequences. It led to the formation of strong, legally protected labor monopolies through the 1935 National Labor Relations Act (NLRA), for reasons that are transparently wrong. In its opening salvo, the NLRA laments "[t]he inequality of bargaining power between employees who do not possess full freedom of association or actual liberty of contract, and employers who are organized in the corporate or other forms of ownership association."[19] The words "full" and "actual" are weasel words that are intended to conceal the truth that the ordinary norms of full contractual freedom apply to all workers in a competitive market. In fact, allowing those competitive forces to operate during the pre-1935 period allowed wages to rise, not only for union workers but across the board. The same mindset secured the passage of the Fair Labor Standards Act (FLSA) in 1938, which gave government bureaucrats extensive powers to regulate wages, hours, and overtime.[20] Over the years, the FLSA has extended its reach to ever more classes of employees, including the employees of state governments, an enlargement of purview that was sustained only after a major constitutional battle that resulted in yet another victory of expanded federal power.[21] Passage of the act ushered in a variety of restrictions that forced government bureaucrats to decide how to value all noncash forms of compensation, to give some authoritative definition of what counts as an "hour," and to develop norms for when overtime is appropriate.[22]

At one level, the inquiry looks innocent, because we all have over-broad mental pictures of how we think labor markets operate. But the infinite variety of business arrangements often leads to industrial practices that do not jibe with the strong preconception that overtime work is necessarily more arduous than regular labor. This clash between common sense and the FLSA surfaced early, in *Skidmore v. Swift & Co.*

(1944),[23] which asked how to apply the overtime rules to employees who remained on call on company premises, ready to answer fire alarms. Prior to the FLSA, the Swift Company had paid its overtime workers a low base wage, which let them play or sleep on the job. It then paid larger sums on a piecework basis for answering alarms. That two-tier pay schedule appears to track the business interests of both parties. But it does not fit into the procrustean bed that requires time-and-a-half wages for overtime work. This one example among many reveals a common difficulty with labor legislation—namely, how it forces the atypical case into the dominant pattern, which may make no sense.

Faced with the dilemma, Justice Robert H. Jackson deferred in *Swift* to the administrative decision that gave overtime for waking but not sleeping activities, because he found that its judgment had "the power to persuade." Why this qualified vote of deference? Because there is no sensible way to answer the question within the framework of the statute. At that point, it is better for a justice to hide behind the judgment of a conscientious administrator in a flawed statutory system than to strike out on one's own. Once again, the willingness to allow public oversight where none is needed creates ad hoc decisions that are, in the end, utterly inconsistent with any clear sense of the rule of law.

Modern Applications

These overtime rules of course raise far more problems than just classification. Someone has to decide what the wages will be, whether to grant exemptions to certain individuals, and, if so, to which ones. The overall effect is typically to push wages to above-market levels that create some—but not too much—unemployment. Yet these calculations can also misfire. For example, recent congressional legislation mandated minimum-wage increases of $0.70 per hour for 2007, 2008, and 2009, and raised the minimum wage by more than 40 percent in two years.[24] That statutory scheme was passed before the contraction in labor markets following the financial dislocations of 2008. But the rigidities in the legislative process gave rise to a spike in teenage unemployment as real wages tended to drop in a period of no inflation, thereby putting the dollar minimum into play far more often than was anticipated.[25]

Similar rigidities are built into the system of collective bargaining in the United States, under which the National Labor Relations Act turns some competitive labor markets into monopolistic ones, by imposing a statutory duty on employers to bargain with an exclusive union representative of a bargaining unit, chosen typically by secret-ballot election under NLRB supervision.[26] The inexorable downward spiral of the domestic automobile industry is attributable in large measure to the inability to make appropriate downward wage adjustments in the face of foreign competition and loss of consumer confidence. Thirty years ago, General Motors had 500,000 workers. By the time of its bankruptcy, its workforce, both salaried (23,000) and hourly (38,000), had fallen to a total of around 61,000. The betting here is that even the large federal bailout, which bent every rule of bankruptcy to support the retired United Auto Workers, will have to struggle to keep a marginal firm alive. Just that result has to be expected when public coercion displaces mutual exchange.

Instead of backing off regulation, however, the latest iteration of progressive thought has pushed for still more government coercion, again with massive amounts of delegation. Thus, the formerly proposed—but now moribund—Employee Free Choice Act (EFCA) has three major provisions.[27] The first seeks to expedite union elections and to stiffen the penalties against employers who speak out against unions during an organization campaign. The sanctions against union misbehavior were left untouched. It is well known that sentiments tend to shift against unions during the course of an organization drive, which means that it is in the interests of unions to have quickie elections before the employer is given a chance to speak. Right now that speech is heavily circumscribed, such that an employer cannot make a threat or promise a benefit during these campaigns.[28] Yet even so, accurate statements of what happens when other firms have become uncompetitive usually work to dissuade many workers from signing up for a union.

The possible wage increase in the short run is more than offset by duties of union membership and the risk that the employer will shutter or shrink his business.

The second proposal substitutes a card check system for the secret-ballot election in union recognition disputes. The union argument is that elections are subject to employer coercion, which surely happens in some, but not many, elections. That argument ignores, of course, the use of all sorts of coercion in the opposite direction, much of which does not involve the internal organization campaigns, but instead strives to use pickets to attract negative publicity to a unionized firm, to use zoning laws to block the business activities of firms subject to union drives, or to take advantage of regulatory schemes that require government officials to act in response to citizen complaints, regardless of when filed. Against this background, card check allows union organizers to waylay workers off-premises in order to pressure them into signing cards that unions can hold, but need not return. The full protection of the secret ballot against all forms of coercion from both sides is effectively removed from the equation.

So why the push to revise labor law in favor of greater government control? The main reason is not that management bludgeons workers. It is that management has a lot to say about the failures of other unionized firms to keep up with the competition, in light of the massive reduction in union membership in such industries as autos and steel. There is no huge evident bias in the conduct of new elections, which divide about evenly over the small units typically in contention. Labor tends to win a few more elections. But employers tend to win in the larger units. The real union losses come from attrition in industries rendered vulnerable to nonunion competition, such as the automotive and steel industries.

The third portion of the EFCA program calls for a system of mandatory arbitration under an initial two-year "contract," which is binding if the parties bargain to an impasse. As is typical of coercive schemes, that bargaining process is on a collision course with rule-of-law concerns. No statute can specify the full terms of any labor contract, let alone over the vast range of areas in which such contracts have to be negotiated. The only way to run this scheme is to delegate the business of sorting out individual conduct to administrative bodies, in this instance to panels appointed by the Federal Mediation and Conciliation Service, situated in the Department of Labor. There are obvious rule-of-law concerns with these institutional arrangements. The risk of bias is manifest, given that political operatives control all key positions in the process. Arbitrariness is likely to occur because no one—not even individuals who specialize in compulsory arbitration in the public sector—has the slightest clue how to impose agreements on ordinary businesses regarding the ways they are managed, transformed, merged, bought, and sold. Nonetheless, these arguably partisan panels, on the basis of zero institutional knowledge, would be authorized to set out the provisions for all aspects of complex bargaining agreements, in the total absence of any standards for drafting these agreements. The risk of excessive delegation is also apparent. Finally, there is no protection against ruinous terms. Even the prospect of passing this legislation would surely discourage the formation of new businesses and encourage established businesses to shift to capital-intensive strategies. As of this writing, all long-term employment projections keep the unemployment rates for full-time workers above 8 percent, perhaps as high as 10 percent. These projections hold true even for those who foresee some modest overall economic recovery in the next few years. The explanation does not lie in any deep macroeconomic theory, however fashionable those explanations are among those who wrongly see the Federal Reserve Board's control over the money supply as the key to our employment woes.[29] It rests on the simple point that the current impediments to job formation won't disappear when public interventions are poised to undercut private job formation. Indeed, in the first year of the Obama administration, the ongoing risk of the EFCA probably had an immediate negative effect on employment, given the uncertainty over the future labor market. Ultimately, we see the power of the classical liberal maxim, "Cooperation yes, coercion no."

9

Positive-Sum Projects

Maximizing Surplus

The accounts of both private property and liberty of contract in their separate ways have as their minimum condition blocking forms of government action that shrink the overall size of the pie. Toward that end, it becomes appropriate to strike down legislation that prevents the gains from trade in consensual arrangements. Likewise, in connection with the operation of state coercion, the initial function of the system invokes a strong just-compensation principle to block negative-sum projects that should not be undertaken in the first place. If the winners cannot pay off the losers and come out ahead, they will abandon their own programs. One of the great purposes of the just-compensation requirement is to block those transactions that should not be undertaken at all, just as one of the great purposes of voluntary markets is to weed out private exchanges which cost more to organize than they are worth.

A complete analysis of property rights, however, must go one step
further by developing a coherent program to address those public-
coerced positive-sum projects that deserve to go forward. On these, the
standard rules of just compensation do not explain how to allocate anticipated gains among all possible claimants. Consider a project with
ten individuals, identically situated, that generates a social surplus of
100. How should that gain be divided? If everything is left up for grabs,
factional intrigue could easily dissipate the entire surplus. Yet the basic
just-compensation requirement leaves any allocation of the gains untouched, so long as no stakeholder is made worse off by the new project.
We need rules that both avoid losses and *maximize* cooperative gain.

But how? Suppose that the government must place a new road
through a small community, dividing it in two. Half the residents are on
one side of the projected path, and half are on the other side. All of
them own identical lots, each of which is 200 feet deep. On completion,
the road will be 50 feet wide, and all property owners must have direct
access to it. No features of topography influence costs. Assume that all
construction costs are divided equally. What route should be chosen?
The road could be built exclusively on the land of the owners on one
side while abutting both; or it could be built right down the middle; or
the state could take 15 feet of land from one side and 35 from the other.
No matter which permutation is taken, all parties are better off with the
road than without it. The amount of the gain for each owner, however,
depends on the road's location. The owner who retains only 150 feet of
land will see his value increase by, say, $100, while those on the other
side of the road, who retain all their land, will see their values increase
by $250. For each foot the road moves, the values on both sides increase
or decrease respectively by 1 unit, so that the total gains of $350 are con-
stant regardless of the road's location.

In this austere hypothetical, the location of the road is a matter of
profound social indifference. Therefore, if the only binding legal constraint were the just-compensation rule, no abutting owner would be

either compensated or taxed, no matter where the road was located within the 100-foot band. The property rights thus become indefinite, giving each party the incentive to lobby to have a larger fraction of the road built on the far side of the property. A full-compensation rule for the loss of land value cancels out all payments under the "fair" solution, which takes 25 feet of land from each owner. But the payments do not even out when 35 feet are taken from the lots on one side and 15 feet from those on the other: now each member of the first group of owners contributes $70, while each member of the second group contributes $30. But let the courts require $20 in payment from the members of the latter group to the former, and the lobbying ceases because the returns to all are the same regardless of where the road gets located. This solution is robust, even when distinctive topological features come into play. Thus, if the uneven terrain makes it cheaper to build on one side than on the other, this extra-compensation requirement leads both sides to pick the ideal site in order to economize on the shared costs of construction. Here is a case in which the unambiguous reduction in state discretion by imposing the payment requirement improves the performance overall, even after the just-compensation requirement is satisfied.

Exactions

Another threat to the creation of social surplus arises from the common practice of attaching exactions for new construction permits. Today, local governments often give building permits only to developers who agree to donate some land for a park or school or museum,[1] to refurbish a nearby train station, or to allow the public to claim a lateral easement to walk to and fro in front of their property.[2] In the environmental context, landowners may fill in designated wetlands only if they "mitigate" the environmental loss by devoting other lands—which they may purchase, if necessary—exclusively to environmental purposes.[3]

Within the current legal system—but only there—these exactions serve a useful function. They reduce the tax burdens otherwise charged to current residents, who often find themselves in a no-lose situation, at least in the short run. If the conditions are accepted, they receive free goods paid for by new entrants. If they are denied, the low densities of the neighborhood are preserved. Today, this exaction game goes on largely without judicial supervision. Two Supreme Court cases, however, hinted at possible limits on the power of local governments to issue permits in exchange for favors. In the first, the court held that the local government could not make the granting of a permit conditional on the owner's granting the government a lateral easement across the front of his property for the benefit of the public at large.[4] In the second, it held that the local government could not refuse to allow for an expanded parking lot unless the owner allowed for the construction of a bike path and a flood control system on her land.[5] Both decisions were right because in neither situation was the exaction done for one of the two legitimate reasons: either to offset a benefit conferred upon the landowner, or to offset a cost that the landowner imposed upon others. In essence, in these cases the public law followed the private law of restitution (a theory designed to prevent unjust enrichment in noncontractual cases or in tort).

Unfortunately, those restrained rulings have lost all of their pop because of judicial nullification in the lower federal and all state courts, as judges have used their ingenuity to find some legitimate purpose for every condition attached to particular permits.[6] And how? By deviating from the classical liberal definition of harm. In its stead, the judges deploy the expanded definitions of harm, which are so congenial to the philosophy of the modern welfare state, to get the discretion that allows them to proceed unimpeded. Remember that if the major enemy of all development is delay, the right to sue (and lose) for improper government action is futile at best. Thus, constant diplomacy becomes the order of the day when property rights become soft.

The standard defense of this common practice rests on a seductive misapplication of the principle of freedom of contract. The landowner values the right to receive the permit more than he does the exaction in cash or kind. The local government values the receipt of the exaction or cash more than it dislikes the new construction. Both sides are better off, so why not seal the deal? Because this bargaining process does not explain where the government got the right to hold up the project in the first place. If the neighbors would have to pay to prevent the wetland from being filled in, then the government should pay, as well. But if they would have to buy the right to keep a wetland in place, which is the normal rule, the state should do so, as well. The decline in the protection of property rights has, however, reversed the ordinary rules by allowing established citizens to unload the common expenses of running a community on the newcomers. In essence, land use exactions allow local governments to *sell back* to landowners their common-law rights of use and development that they had just taken by regulation.

The difficulty with this mitigation policy is that it ducks the fundamental question of initial entitlements, and thus can easily lead to the seizure of property that is worth more in private hands than in public ones. A landowner will surrender an easement that costs it $50,000 to get a building permit with a value of $250,000. But the bundled transaction is socially inefficient if the easement is worth only $30,000 to the public. Separate the exaction from the permit and the state won't buy the easement, given the net social cost of $20,000.

Strategic bundling thus prevents a fair valuation of assets. Yet developers caught by the current rules eagerly pay these exactions in order to buy off community opposition in a legal regime devoid of property rights. Once the deal is struck, the community leaders that previously fought the new development now defend it ferociously against future opponents. Unfortunately, many worthwhile projects fail at this juncture because their promised gains do not leave enough extra wealth to placate potential opponents. An exaction thus produces the same type of resource distortion that other ad hoc taxes create, by *selectively* hitting some developers while giving their competitors an easier time. The only way to prevent abuse is to tie the use of exactions to the standard police power justifications. Exactions tailored to deal with nuisance-like harms or to prevent the overload of public roads pass muster. Those to fund new schools, art museums, and subway stations do not. Here are some instances of how the distinction works. In *Kaiser Aetna v. United States* (1979),[7] the Supreme Court, without using the phrase "unconstitutional conditions," held that the United States could not prevent boats docked at a private marina from entering public waters when the marina refused to allow free entry to all boats into its private waters. Rightly or otherwise, the owner of land could keep the world from parking in his driveway. Nor could California insist that all private carriers that used its highways had to accept regulation as common carriers, when the state has no monopoly power.[8] Nor, more controversially, should the state keep privately operated jitneys off public roads solely because they compete with public transit lines and their union employees.[9] Safety justifications are one thing. Anticompetitive motivations are another. Congestion may be regulated, for example, by evenhanded rules that give no priority to the first user of the roads. But exclusion in favor of incumbents is impermissible.

The cardinal distinction between safety and monopoly regulation looms equally large in interstate contexts. Thus, the Massachusetts high court upheld a rule that required any out-of-state driver on public highways to litigate road accident cases within the state.[10] It would be a massive inconvenience to allow litigation elsewhere if all the relevant facts and evidence were local, and all parties to the dispute had a least some temporary presence in the state. Yet by the same token, Massachusetts should not be able to allow out-of-state persons to use its highways only if they agreed to litigate their divorces in state court. To highlight the profound structural difference between these two cases, just ask what would happen if all states adopted identical rules. Litigating accidents in the place of their occurrence would create no undue advantage. The more states that followed the rule, the better the tort system would become. But no person should be required to agree to litigate her divorce in each state through which she has traveled. The more states that adopted that rule, the more acute the conflicts would be among the states, and the more inconsistent the demands of all private parties. The rival claims in the divorce setting would be inconsistent, not complementary, so that all would have to be rejected.

Political and Religious Liberties

The doctrine of unconstitutional conditions is not, moreover, limited solely to cases that involve highways or other public facilities in which only economic matters are at stake. That doctrine also applies to all sorts of public forums when personal interests in freedom of association or political and religious liberty are at stake as well. The basic rule here is one that takes the following form. All public facilities should, as a first approximation, be open to all people. In most instances, they must therefore be open to people who wish to exercise their right to exclude others from their ventures. That condition surely holds, for it is improper for the state to say that it will let a person drive on the public roads only if he agrees to carry unwanted passengers for free. It also holds when, for example, a Catholic organization wishes to exclude gay-rights advocates from its float during a St. Patrick's Day Parade, as happened in *Hurley v. Irish-American Gay, Lesbian and Bisexual Group* (1995).[11] The Supreme Court rightly held that, even on public property, the associational rights of the church trumped the desire of the gay-rights group to join the parade, even in the teeth of a state antidiscrimination law that made it illegal to discriminate on grounds of sexual orientation.[12]

That decision took some high-stepping because of the entrenched (if unsound) distinction between ordinary rights of association in economic matters and similar rights of association in matters of religious or political expression. The dominant modern opinion, fully accepted in the Supreme Court,[13] applies two different sets of rules to the two different types of organization, an approach that necessitates drawing some awkward line between them. Yet the court even held that the freedom-

of-association norm trumped the antidiscrimination norm on these expressive activities. The broader view holds that an antidiscrimination
rule should be used only as a counterweight to monopoly power, which
some private organizations sometimes possess but which the state routinely exercises.

The key point here is that so long as the state does have that monopoly power, its activities must be subject to strong correlative limitations. Accordingly, the state that cannot enforce its position through
legislation against individuals on private property cannot enforce them
by excluding them from public property, given the evident dangers from
this use of monopoly power. At this point, the somewhat surprising
conclusion is that, as a first approximation, the state as the operator of
most public facilities has no greater right of regulation as an owner of
public facilities than it does as a regulator of private ones. Political discretion is limited in ways that induce public performance consistent
with the rule of law. In effect, the basic principle says that ordinary private common carriers have to take all customers on reasonable and nondiscriminatory terms. So, too, does the state when it operates as a common carrier in the maintenance of public facilities and in the operation
of systems of public transportation.

Yet there are surely limits to this principle in those cases in which
the state is not running a common carrier, but acting in discharge of its
own duties of public administration. The rule that allows all individuals
to ride on a public bus does not guarantee them access to the Pentagon
War Room. The difficult questions therefore arise when certain forums
are limited in their use on some occasions but not on others in cases
that involve "a limited public forum." Just that issue came to a head in
the Supreme Court case of *Christian Legal Society Chapter of the University of California Hastings College of the Law v. Martinez* (2010),[14] where
the question was whether Hastings College could prevent members of
the Christian Legal Society (CLS) from using its rooms and other facilities, solely because Hastings was strongly opposed to CLS's opposition
to a variety of homosexual-rights issues. The correct view in this case
draws a distinction between Hastings as a manager of its own business

and Hastings as the owner of a limited public facility that it makes available to all students on its own terms. Unlike the situation with public roads, Hastings has no obligation to admit all comers to its facilities when its classrooms are in use. Indeed, it has no obligation to allow all of its student organizations to use the college's facilities for their own purposes when those facilities are not being used by the college itself. But what Hastings cannot do is to pick and choose among the student groups according to their political and religious viewpoints.

Unfortunately, Justice Ruth Bader Ginsburg, writing for the court, missed that point; she saw no reason to apply the doctrine of unconstitutional conditions in the first place. Instead, she drew precisely the wrong distinction when she held that even if the state could not prosecute CLS for its views, it ran into no constitutional obstacle so long as it "merely" withheld a benefit from the disfavored group. The decision thereby revived the long-discredited "right/privilege distinction" that for many years marred this area of law.[15] In Justice Ginsburg's view, so long as Hastings College did not single out religious groups for special dispensation under its nondiscrimination policy, Hastings could impose that policy across the board, no matter how disparate its impact on CLS. Yet this illiberal policy does exactly what the rule of law contravenes, by allowing a level of discretion to public officials which they do not need in order to administer the essential educational functions of their home institutions. This situation illustrates how a dominant faction may use its power to exclude for the purpose of beating up a small fringe group that cannot defend itself in the political process. One wonders about the soundness of a court that fully understands the need to protect the on-campus rights of the Students for a Democratic Society, but fails to see the same necessity for a group whose own views are rather distinct from its own.

Summing Up

The doctrine of unconstitutional conditions is a protean doctrine, untethered from any particular substantive area of law. It applies whenever and wherever the state claims special powers to regulate under its full range of permit and regulatory powers. As such, this doctrine backstops the rule of law on both individual and structural issues by protecting positive-sum projects from political intrigue. To be sure, discussion of rent-seeking and Prisoner's Dilemma games may at first seem out of place in any discussion of constitutional law. But it is not. The only way to limit state discretion is through a strong system of property rights that stops negative-sum games and creates definite property rights in positive-sum games. It is to these ends that the classic rules on takings and just compensation are dedicated.

10

Redistribution Last

The overall substantive picture of the classical liberal view is still incomplete, because it has thus far omitted discussion of one central practice of the modern welfare state: redistribution of wealth to offset disadvantages from birth, ill fortune, or social position. Within the classical liberal framework, the case for redistribution, at least through voluntary transfers, rests on overtly welfarist grounds. It is widely (and correctly) assumed that individuals derive diminishing marginal utility from additional units of wealth. Some equalization of wealth therefore should, all else being equal, increase the overall levels of social utility from the same amount of wealth. That is why voluntary charitable work for the poor long preceded the advent of state welfare programs. Strong defenders of property rights and the rule of law should not therefore be indifferent to manifest imbalances of wealth. Historically, they never were. Before the clear separation of the state from the extended family, redistribution was a powerful and persistent fact of life. Given the normal and predictable fluctuations in agricultural production alone, those individuals who earned enough to stay above the subsistence line in one period could easily fall below it in the next period.

In this context, redistribution to persons in need thus looks less like a one-shot transfer from A to B, and rather more like part of an informal but comprehensive insurance scheme. Confining redistribution to cases of "extreme want"[1] shows the limited but vital role that such restrictions played in earlier centuries, when there was an equally pressing need to preserve incentives for productive labor. A farmer might be asked to leave his gleanings from the harvest for poor people to collect. Using a form of in-kind assistance had three powerful consequences. First, it tended to focus redistribution to high-return cases where survival was very much at issue, and away from cases where all persons had enough wealth to be above the starvation level. If individual survival requires 5 units of resources, redistribution of 2 units from someone who has 9 to someone with 3 matters. Even if one unit of wealth disappears in the transfer, at 6 units and 5 units, two people live instead of one. Conversely, shifting 200 units from someone who has 900 to someone who has 300 produces far less—if any—social gain, because both individuals survive whether or not these transfers are made. The ratios matter less than the totals. Second, any gleanings were limited in amount and were proportionate, roughly speaking, to the levels of production. Third, the recipient had to collect the gleanings, and could not rely on a cash payment that required no work. These de facto restrictions held down the level of redistribution to preserve incentives for production.

In addition, earlier societies developed a strong tradition of "imperfect obligations" to help the poor, either directly or through intermediaries. The "imperfect" nature of the obligation kept redistribution out of the legal system and put it in the hands of voluntary private organizations like churches, foundling homes, and hospitals, which in most cases could better monitor the recipients' behavior than any detached public agency. Often, the aid was directed to persons with identifiable conditions such as malnutrition, blindness, and deafness, which few individuals incur specifically in order to receive some modest public aid. Using such systems as public hospital wards capitalized on these features to keep the welfare system small. These inelegant solutions were susceptible to insensitive application in individual cases. But they did make real inroads into the insistent problem of human subsistence in times when the material resource base was far smaller than it is today.

In sum, there is surely a case for melding these elements into a comprehensive system, but not so as to overwhelm the productive features of voluntary exchange and public taxation. The best solution to the problem of unequal wealth distribution is economic growth that reduces the size of the problem by expanding the size of the pie. The banner that captures this program is "redistribution last," which proposes a priority list of social reforms. First, remove the various obstacles that the system places in the path of voluntary improvement by way of excessive regulation or taxation. Once those problems are solved, then attack the (fewer) pockets of poverty that remain. It is much easier to accomplish modest redistribution off a large wealth base than to engage in extensive redistribution off a small wealth base. No rule-of-law considerations demand this approach. But the most robust conception of the rule of law is fully consistent with it.

The role of redistribution becomes inescapably broader under the modern administrative state. In this context, the combination of broad agency delegation and weak property rights leaves the amounts and objectives of redistribution at the mercy of political pressures. No longer is its object to use transfers that take advantage of the diminishing marginal utility of wealth by transferring resources from rich to poor. The careful efforts to limit redistribution to one sensible purpose are displaced by a plethora of dubious ends that work at cross-purposes with that one classical liberal theme. Everyone is now entitled to jump on the public bandwagon because of society's ability to manufacture in the political arena all sorts of positive rights to jobs, health, education, and living wages. It is critical to note, however, that none of these positive rights can have any of the three attributes that earlier were intimately connected with common-law rules of private property (see Chapter 5, above).

First, none of the systems can be *universal*. Now that mutual forbearance on invasion is not the end, individuals have to be broken up into classes; some of them are eligible to receive benefits and others are required to give. Which persons fall into which classes always raises politically contestable questions because of the endless number of positive rights that can claim support. The very individuals who are recipients under one version of the theory are payers under another version. The question of who receives is often separated from the question of who pays. One illustration of this was how Virginia funded its program for no-fault benefits to newborns injured by human actions before or during childbirth: the funds were raised through taxes on laundromats and similar facilities. Trade wars, in their own way, have the same random connection. These arise precisely because governments are willing to limit the rights of disposition normally found in the bundle of domestic- and foreign-property rights, so that these questions are not just a matter of high-level negotiations between governments, unconnected with issues of private rights. Let American beef be excluded from some overseas nation, and we can exclude draperies or paper clips in exchange. The tight connections between the wrongdoer and the victim that are a feature of the corrective-justice view of tort law vanish when state power is thrown into the mix. In the end, the crazy-quilt pattern of net transfers could easily cancel out so that everyone comes out a loser.

Second, none of these political chits is *scalable*. Every time new people move in or out of the jurisdiction, the credits and debits are thrown out of alignment, so that someone has to determine eligibility, raise taxes, cut benefits, or some combination of the above, with all the attendant uncertainties of the political process. This point has become evident with the current economic malaise that has threatened the solvency of key states such as California, New York, and Illinois, which today CEOs rank in this order as the worst three states in the nation for their receptivity to business.[2] The usual pattern is to think of high taxes as a way to satisfy state obligations to those in-groups (think public union pensions) to whom the revenue is owed. But at the state level, at least, the exit rights matter, so that high-income people can and will flee jurisdictions that make aggressive use of their taxing power, which is why these states constantly seek federal bailouts, which then allow irresponsible ongoing fiscal management.[3] Therefore, change wealth levels and a constant readjustment is needed in order to balance accounts. The turmoil never occurs with the creation and protection of negative rights.

The efforts to provide universal health care often founder on just this insight. Here is one variation. This nation is too large to administer as a single whole, so that redistribution through government programs is tied to location. In a market system, the class of insureds does not matter for the calculation of the premium, which in all cases is equal to the expected cost of the coverage plus an allowance for the administrative load. But once there are built-in cross-subsidies within a given geographic region, the boundaries of the district matter because persons located in poor health districts pay far greater premiums than do those with the identical personal attributes who are located in low-risk districts.[4] At this point, a political fight ensues to draw favorable boundaries, which dissipates wealth without creating any social improvement. Community rating plans that put men and women (who have different risks at different ages) and young and old in the same pool also create that system of cross-subsidies, which results either in the withdrawal from the pool of low-risk persons or forced mandates to keep them in. These are not small or technical problems. They dog every single effort to mandate insurance or welfare pools.

Third, the assignment of positive rights is not *stable* against changes in overall wealth. What works in one locale or area won't work in another. Thus, constitutions that seek to mandate these positive rights are never able to make them "enforceable," in the strong sense of that word. Instead, the constitutional right gets enforced as a judicial command to the legislature, which in turn has to decide which rights are sustainable in which economic conditions. That process is not, however, a free lunch, for the very act of decision invites political intrigue that imposes high costs, often without clear knowledge as to whether the state-determined allocations generate a distributional gain that can offset the unambiguous social losses from a smaller pie.

All of these disadvantages are cumulative, but the system is often tolerated by the transparent ruse that the duties of payment fall on the state rather than on the individuals who are taxed or regulated to fund these obligations. The allocative losses from redistribution are usually ignored, often due to the implicit assumption that a dollar taken from one results in a dollar given to another. That assumption overlooks the decline in overall wealth attributable to factional struggles and administrative costs. Even harsher words should be directed to the perverse patterns of redistribution brought on, for example, by an endless array of corporate subsidies that provide government support to the financially fortunate, who should instead be encouraged to engage in pie-expanding activities. Under modern schemes of government, poor-to-rich redistribution is as likely as the opposite.

Nor are the patterns sustainable in the long haul, because of the endless pressure to push benefits forward and to defer costs. By design, Social Security included in its first round of payments initial enrollees who had made no contribution to the program. The funding imbalances in the initial allocation got built into what can only be called a government-sponsored Ponzi scheme, whose unfunded obligations continued to grow unchecked notwithstanding the constant warnings of impending doom. Today's only serious debate over Social Security, Medicare (with its new Part D on prescription drugs), and Medicaid is not whether they will become insolvent, but when that will happen, and what horrific dislocations will follow.

The situation has deteriorated to such an extent that in the 2010 Medicare Annual Report, the government's own actuary, Richard S. Foster, disavowed the relatively rosy projections made in the report, on the ground that they did not take into account the fact that Congress would routinely restore the cuts in physician's fees in order to prevent an immediate implosion of a system that was badly run and overwhelmed with too many rights chasing too few resources. Thus, Foster wrote, "the financial projections shown in this report for Medicare do not represent a reasonable expectation for actual program operations in either the short range (as a result of the unsustainable reductions in physician payment rates) or the long range (because of the strong likelihood that the statutory reductions in price updates for most categories of Medicare provider services will not be viable)."[5] The projections became only more dire in 2011, when government actuaries again repeated their urgent warnings about the unsustainability of the Medicare program.[6] More generally, programs of positive rights have no built-in bias toward sustainability. In passing, it is worth noting that the only portion of this system that has outperformed projections is Part D, which also is the only portion of the program that relies on market incentives to control costs.

The United States—and for similar reasons, much of western Europe—are now at a critical juncture: they are caught between two powerful social forces that are not easily reconciled. On the one hand, enormous pressures mount in bad times to expand the level of transfer payments to the less fortunate—and everyone else. The current conversation centers on refundable tax credits, which are disguised welfare payments to individuals who have already been insulated from all obligations under the income tax. Yet on the other side, there are proposals now afoot, especially on labor and health issues, to shrink the national resource base by placing new burdens on voluntary exchange. The dominant views of the current democratic health care programs heavily subsidize health care consumption, impose onerous regulations to keep these subsidies from flowing to a wide range of health care providers, and tax and regulate everyone, both within and outside the favored state exchanges used to administer the health care system.

No government, however, can be all things to all people. Simple math indicates that any nation that tries to increase redistribution while reducing productivity is heading, at best, for a prolonged period of stagflation, and more likely for a crash of major proportions. There are, of course, sensible voices that counsel against these reckless programs. Political prudence, however, may not be sufficient to forestall the political pressures that move so strongly in the opposite direction. This potential economic meltdown could never happen within a classical liberal framework that rests on the twin pillars of limited administrative discretion and strong property rights.

Against this background, the right attitude on redistribution is not to rule it out of bounds on first principles, when in fact there is considerable (but not unlimited) public support for these programs. Rather, the better approach is to adopt the philosophy of "redistribution last."[7] The overall strategy is as follows. First, make sure that the productive side of the economy is in good shape; it should work through open competition and vibrant markets to raise the level of overall wealth, including that acquired by the least fortunate in society. Once that base is preserved, the scope of redistributive policies can be accordingly reduced, given that a large resource base is coupled with a lower level of need. In this environment, the reduced burden allows voluntary contributions to pick up more of the slack, which further reduces the need for public funding. In stark contrast, the current entitlement cycle drives the relationship between production and redistribution in the wrong direction, stretching fewer resources to meet ever-larger political demands. The feared—and most likely—result of this vicious circle is that the bubble that has burst in the real estate markets will burst elsewhere, due to entitlement programs that consume a disproportionate fraction of the national wealth. The price for our rejection of the rule of law and strong property rights is steep indeed.

11

The Rule of Law Diminished

Administrative Law in the Progressive Era

Thus far, I have explained how classical liberal principles link the rule of law and the system of private property into a harmonious whole. In addition, I have sought to explain why the alternative progressive synthesis necessarily introduces new levels of discretion for public officials in applying the substantive law. At this point, we must circle back to see how these modern transformations of the rules of property and contract have placed undue pressure on the rule of law. These changes, moreover, have also placed great responsibilities on public administration that force it to make far more painful choices. The signs of tension are most evident in the financial crisis that began in mid-2008 and has yet to run its course. Even with the contentious passage of the Democratic health care and financial initiatives, it now seems clear that for the moment the march of the administrative state has not yet waned, given that new initiatives on global warming, labor markets, and financial regulation wait in the wings. I shall turn to those laws in somewhat greater detail in the next chapter. For the moment, let us explore the frame of mind that is needed to bring about those innovations in the first place. The basic explanation is none too difficult to identify. The onslaught of administrative regulation has gained traction because modern constitutional and political theory rejects the presumption of distrust in government. This expansion of the government's purview undoes virtually all of the procedural and structural features of the classical system:[1] unbiased decisionmaking, judicial review of administrative actions on matters of fact and law, and retroactivity. To be clear, the criticism here is not that all forms of public administration necessarily fail to meet these rudimentary requirements of the rule of law. Rather, it is that as the scope of government activities increases, the far-flung nature of these activities leads to a great desire to take shortcuts in regulation, such that the older protections are treated as obstructions against the march of progress, and not as protections of individual rights. Ironically, the new rights explosion often operates to let private individuals block key traditional government functions on such critical matters as constructing roads and maintaining public lands, where the appropriate need for managerial discretion is curtailed. These pathologies are not just historical curiosities. They are also very much in play in dealing with many of the key issues on the two signal pieces of legislation in the Obama administration: the health care bill and the Dodd-Frank financial reforms. I shall consider these in the next chapter, after laying out the key developments of the administrative transformation.

Bias

The mass of business affairs brought before the administrative state sorely tests its ability to resolve disputes before impartial judges under basic rules of general application. Much modern legislation creates ex-

plicit preferences for employees, tenants, or consumers that are at odds
with the basic impersonal principles of common law that need identify
people only as A, B, or C. This effort to create rules for each party to
each different type of relationship necessarily confers more discretion
on public officials. That discretion has more bite because, once those
rules are laid down, it is no longer possible for the parties to vary them
by private agreement. One-size-fits-all commands dominate tailored arrangements. Worse still, the parties who are selected to administer these
systems are chosen for their views on one topic only, which could easily lead to polarization of opinions that dominates any supposed expertise.

Ironically, however, individuals receive less protection before administrative tribunals than they do in courts. To be sure, we still have
the time-honored stricture that prohibits a judge or decisionmaker from
having a financial stake in the outcome of litigation. But the modern
administrative rules invite a weaker form of bias by relaxing the structural protections of the separation of powers.[2] More specifically, it is
now permissible to combine investigative and adjudicative functions in
the same persons. At this point, the usual separation of functions that
applies in judicial trials is no longer present. Any perceptions which
are created in the initial investigative stage are therefore likely to carry
through to adjudication. It is just this form of precommitment that
leads to the separation of prosecutors from judges in ordinary criminal
cases, and which also leads in well-run offices to a level of internal oversight that works hard to root out all implicit biases that lurk throughout
the system.[3]

A second source of bias arises in the administrative state because the
broad declarations of legislative purpose give vast amounts of delegated
authority to administrative agents, who then are free to shape policy
under the guise of its implementation, with none of the safeguards of
democratic deliberation. The original constitutional scheme sought to
control these delegations of power in part by parceling out all the powers of the federal government among the legislative, executive, and judi-

cial branches, leaving no explicit place for independent administrative agencies. That structural arrangement offered a de facto constraint on the expansion of federal power because of the reluctance of Congress to give a long-term blank check to the President.

But the risk of bias is evident in any statute that contains specific subject-matter delegations. That danger is evident, for example, in the National Labor Relations Act of 1935.[4] It looks odd, of course, to find explicit party affiliation requirements on a neutral board whose members are appointed for their supposed expertise on labor issues. But since the National Labor Relations Board (NLRB) only reviews management/ union issues, it is easy to typecast all board members as liberal or conservative. So politics comes in on the ground floor. By statute, the head of the NLRB is appointed by the President from his own political party. By custom, the remaining members of the board are divided equally by political party. In practice, paired nominations are the norm: no Republican can be confirmed without a Democrat, and vice versa. As of February 2010, the NLRB was down to two members, one from each party, because the required matchups could not get through Congress. It is thus quite possible that the board cannot operate at all for want of a quorum, an issue that has divided the lower courts and which now seems headed for the Supreme Court.[5]

The polarization of the board is made more dangerous because of its broad grants of delegated authority that do not crystallize into particular rules. National labor law requires the NLRB to determine the membership of "bargaining units" for the purposes of deciding who is eligible to vote in union elections. No territorial principle answers this question, which is necessarily resolved on an ad hoc basis that turns on a host of "factors," each relevant and none decisive. These include the type of union, the history of the unit, its connection to the overall business, the wishes of the workers, and the duties, job skills, and working conditions of the employees.[6] Unit determination is no easy task, as bitter jurisdictional disputes over organizing rights often arise between different rival unions, some of which want to organize along craft lines (electricians, carpenters, etc.) and others along plant lines. Moreover, deciding who is in and who is out often seals the outcome of the election. In the end, the messy facts on the ground frequently induce courts to defer to the NLRB, which in turn defers to organizing unions' choices of bargaining units.[7] So expertise ends up second-best to politics. None of these institutional issues arise when employers are not put under a statutory obligation to bargain in good faith with workers. The level of state coercion needed to keep employers locked in losing labor contracts is thus inconsistent with the rule of law.

Judicial Review of Administrative Action: The Great Inversion

Administrative agencies also impose serious burdens on the judicial bodies that oversee their actions on both matters of fact and questions of law. On this question, the usual attitude in ordinary litigation is to defer to the trier of fact—either the jury, or a judge in a case tried without a jury—on matters of fact, but to review all decisions of law under a de novo standard, which affords no deference to the decision below. That division of labor makes perfectly good sense. Trial judges and juries are better able to evaluate the presentation of evidence for a variety of reasons, but have no comparative advantage in dealing with the larger questions of statutory or contractual interpretation that rely on standardized techniques that do not vary much from case to case and area to area. In these matters, since uniformity to a larger body of law matters, appellate courts, including the Supreme Court in the few cases in which it does intervene, should pay respectful attention to the arguments made below, without having to defer to their judgments.

The rise of the administrative state typically substitutes administrative agencies for the judges and juries that try cases. In many cases, the factual records are dense and difficult to access. Nonetheless, the same distribution of responsibility is called for. There should be some deference to agencies on the matters of fact that are implicated in their decisions. But on matters of law, it is, if anything, all the more important that agencies, whose current membership often has well-defined political agendas, receive no deference on these critical legal questions. The great tragedy of modern administrative law is that it *inverts* this relationship. Too often, courts defer on legal matters that are within their expertise. And yet on matters of fact, they intervene far too aggressively. This last point is especially true in many cases where administrative officials are charged not with the regulation of private business activities, but with running their own affairs. In those situations, the usual standard of liability that is applied in the case of corporate officers and directors should apply here. No one receives carte blanche on matters of behavior in which they have fiduciary duties. But in general, courts should not seek to upset the good faith decisions by administrative agencies charged with the management of public functions. Unfortunately, the lopsided decisions of the Supreme Court have flipped the current legal position, so that intervention on governance matters is routine, while deference on issues of statutory construction, when the government acts as a coercive regulator, is far too common. How did this great inversion take place?

LEGAL QUESTIONS. Administrative decisions put courts on the horns of a real dilemma. Sometimes courts crave the ability to exercise greater control over countless legal matters. At other times, these same courts get overwhelmed by the high volume of business, which leaves them with a profound sense of their own institutional impotence. This second tendency often wins out when courts, fearful of the additional work, give a free pass to the decisions that many administrative bodies make on questions of law. For example, that second tendency won out when, in 1932, the Supreme Court allowed the United States Employee Compensation Commission to decide on the outer limits of its own jurisdiction under the Longshore and Harbor Workers' Compensation Act.[8] The manifest risk that an imperial agency would expand (or unduly contract) its own powers for selfish reasons was not found sufficient to require neutral judicial review of the question. Yet the common view is to downplay this problem by insisting that an "agency construction of its own regulations is entitled to substantial deference." Why?

"[B]ecause applying an agency's regulation to complex or changing circumstances calls upon the agency's unique expertise and policymaking prerogatives, we presume that the power authoritatively to interpret its own regulations is a component of the agency's delegated lawmaking powers."[9] It is easy to expand the scope of the administrative state by looking at government actions through rose-colored goggles.

Unfortunately, this approach can yield uncontested agency flip-flops. Thus, in *Rapanos v. United States*,[10] Congress under the Clean Water Act granted the Army Corps of Engineers the power to make rules governing the "waters of the United States."[11] The original regulations covered waters (not puddles) that did support or were capable of supporting navigation.[12] In response to political pressure, however, the Army Corps abandoned this definition as too narrow, so that by the time of *Rapanos,* the revised definition covered "[a]ll interstate waters including interstate wetlands"; "[a]ll other waters such as intrastate lakes, rivers, streams (including intermittent streams), mudflats, sandflats, wetlands, sloughs, prairie potholes, wet meadows, playa lakes, or natural ponds, the use, degradation or destruction of which could affect interstate or foreign commerce"; "[t]ributaries of [such] waters," and "[w]etlands adjacent to [such] waters [and tributaries] (other than waters that are themselves wetlands)."[13]

The choice of definitions does not involve some fine recalibration of the initial standard. Rather, it tracks a well-documented revolution in environmental sensibilities. No longer does the Army Corps have jurisdiction over a few defined water courses. Instead, it takes a Herculean challenge to pinpoint any state land or water that lies outside the Army Corps's reach. Sailing on open waters does not mean lying beached on a sandflat. Both ordinary language and historical usage point to the narrower definition. No false appeal to deference should cloud the simple definitional inquiry.

It was not to be. Once again, the Supreme Court divided on political lines. Justice Antonin Scalia's tough-minded but accurate reading of the statute in favor of the original narrow definition could not collect a majority of five. The four liberal justices dissented, on the ground that

additional federal power translated into greater environmental protection. Justice Anthony Kennedy's enigmatic fifth vote threw matters into
disarray by insisting that the lower court make ad hoc factual inquiries
to decide how far the waters of the United States run. That fact-dense
inquiry highlights Lon Fuller's fear that unclear mandates could allow a
government agency, here the Army Corps, to impose heavy costs, intol-
erable delays, and possible criminal sanctions on parties seeking permits.[14] The case departs from the classical liberal position that would
allow the Army Corps to enjoin activities only on a showing that the
landowner's actions have either caused or threatened immediate harm
to navigable waters, leaving the states to deal with other forms of nuisance, preferably under the same norm of imminent harm. Yet the current dominant view of the world creates an additional risk of tag-team
concurrent jurisdiction between federal and state agencies, both of
which favor more aggressive enforcement of the environmental laws.
First one, then the other, takes the lead in imposing the regulations in
question, thus resulting in more aggressive state actions than could occur with either agency acting on its own. To be sure, in some cases, federal and state agencies clash over the environmental policy. But it was
no accident that in *Rapanos* thirty-four state environmental agencies
signed an amicus brief in support of extending federal power in this
area. That result bespeaks cooperation, not conflict.

Against this institutional background, the hard institutional question is why any Supreme Court justice would want to leave questions of
statutory interpretation to administrative discretion. Congress itself addressed just this point in the Administrative Procedure Act:

§706. Scope of Review
To the extent necessary to decisions and when presented, the reviewing court shall decide all relevant questions of law, interpret constitutional and statutory provisions, and determine the meaning or
applicability of terms of agency action.[15]

This provision reversed (at the insistence of the Republican Congress after World War II) the earlier New Deal practice of extensive

agency discretion. The issues specified as covered by Section 706 were identical to those that courts handled prior to the rise of the administrative state. But the section itself has had almost no influence whatsoever on the subsequent evolution of the law.

The now regnant pattern of deference in *Rapanos,* however, was derived from the seminal (if misguided) 1984 Supreme Court decision in *Chevron U.S.A., Inc. v. Natural Resources Defense Council, Inc.,*[16] which asked whether a firm could treat multiple smokestacks from a single facility as a "point source" under the Clean Air Act. If so, then the firm could switch output from one portion of its facility to another without first having to laboriously petition the EPA for a permit for making new source pollutants. The Carter administration's narrow definition of "point source" required new permitting, which delayed starting up new plants, which in turn extended the use of older, dirtier plants already in operation—yet another sad illustration of the law of unintended consequences. The Reagan administration's broader "point source" definition avoided that difficulty, but invited an immediate challenge by environmental organizations. Ruth Bader Ginsburg, then a circuit-court judge, held that the new permits were indeed necessary in order to vindicate the statutory purpose of securing clean air.[17] Justice John Paul Stevens's highly influential opinion for the Supreme Court overturned her decision and sustained the change in policy advocated by the Reagan administration—without question, a marked improvement on what had been done in the court below. But Justice Stevens refused to treat the question of statutory construction as a matter of law for the Supreme Court to decide under Section 706, which indeed he never cited, let alone discussed. Instead of interpreting the statute—which would have sustained the agency position—he deferred to the EPA's decision. He got the right result for the wrong reason, by ceding broad interpretive authority in tough cases to agency officials. Just how often and for what reason deference to agencies is appropriate was left unclear. In consequence, we now have a huge cottage industry asking how much deference should be accorded in which cases. The crazy-quilt decisions thus denigrate the judicial process while exposing parties to administrative flip-flops, like the one in *Rapanos,* that wreak havoc with the rule of law.

The only way this result could be avoided is for judges to take the exact opposite position. They should concede—or, better, *insist*—that the vicissitudes of the legislative process will often produce statutes with loose ends. It is easy to use confused language, to make the wrong cross-references, or to equivocate on key statutory provisions. Yet none of that counts as an argument for deference to administrative agencies that have no more skill on interpretive issues than judges, and perhaps less. To be sure, the worse the statute, the higher the error rate in its interpretation. But again, that observation stems from the need to interpret, not from lodging that ultimate responsibility in courts. Of course, administrative agencies with genuine expertise on matters should be able to improve the odds of winning in court, just by presenting arguments whose intellectual power has the power to persuade, without the benefit of any undue *Chevron* deference.

To do otherwise is to invite the worst of agency behaviors. Thus, some years ago, I represented some of the local exchange carriers in matters before the Federal Communication Commission on the knotty question of the respective powers of the federal and state commissions in the administration of the new interconnection standards under the 1996 Federal Telecommunications Act.[18] The details of those disputes, in which the FCC eventually prevailed, are irrelevant here. But the FCC attitude on the regulations that was expressed on that occasion must be repeated literally thousands of times a day as part of the internal deliberations of all sorts of agencies, as well as in their negotiations with outside parties. In response to a query that I made about its statutory construction, I did not receive an argument that my position was wrong for any substantive reason in particular. Rather, I was told that the FCC did not really have to worry about the point because "we have *Chevron* deference."

Note the subtle transformation in the use of this interpretive principle. Everyone was quite sure that the original administrative decision in the *Chevron* dispute was not made on the assumption that the agency had any kind of deference at all. If anything, the presumption was in the opposite direction: meddlesome judges would over-read a statute in order to invalidate the most careful administrative deliberation. But once *Chevron* was on the books, it ceased to operate as an exogenous norm that judges could invoke to interpret a statute passed in blissful ignorance of this particular safety net. Rather, it has become a weapon that is used to jam overly aggressive readings of the statute against various private persons. No longer does an agency have to accommodate its actions to the commands of a statute. Now it need only be able to persuade a court that it has not gone too far beyond the margin of error that the agency receives courtesy of the Supreme Court. Those types of games are not defensible, regardless of the ends they serve. The *Chevron* advantage undercuts any claim for the clarity of language; it lets partisan agencies push the law beyond its natural meaning; and it encourages a kind of judicial skepticism that is nowhere needed. To be sure, the Supreme Court has said, commendably, that it will not allow that deference in cases where the meaning is plain—a stricture that is all to the good, and applied with great effect in many cases. But this second-order move is best understood as a damage control mechanism. Too much damage has already been done by the adoption of a linguistic frame of mind that is all too eager to transfer this responsibility down. It should not be. The responsibility to interpret the law belongs in the end to judges, in both hard and easy cases.

FACTUAL QUESTIONS. Modern administrative law often fails in the opposite direction, by having appellate courts intervene on matters of fact properly left to administrative agencies. In this context, administrative law should follow the distribution of power between judge and jury in ordinary civil litigation. Accordingly, Section 706 of the Administrative Procedure Act says: "The reviewing court shall—(2) hold unlawful and set aside agency action, findings, and conclusions found to be— (A) arbitrary, capricious, an abuse of discretion, or otherwise not in accordance with law."[19] This statutory command requires courts to respect an agency's determination on complex factual questions, such as whether pollution emissions have exceeded some threshold level. In effect, the agency is analogized to the trier of fact in ordinary litigation, be it the jury or the trial judge. Thus, determinations of basic facts are left to the agency until its determination is shown to be "clearly erroneous." That is the standard followed when an injured party seeks either damages or an injunction for a common-law nuisance. No better standard presents itself in an administrative context, given that agencies, like trial judges and juries, have better access to information on factual questions than they do on policy matters.

The law, however, has not played out that way. Instead, the strict judicial oversight for arbitrary and capricious decisions has inverted the original administrative-law scheme. A strong antidevelopment and proregulation view of the world has led courts to meddle unwisely in the government management of public works and public lands. Three prominent cases tell the tale.

First, *Scenic Hudson Preservation Conference v. FPC (I) & (II)*[20] held that the Federal Power Commission (predecessor of the Federal Energy Regulatory Commission) should not have authorized the construction of a new hydroelectric project at Storm King Mountain, located on the west side of the Hudson River, north of New York City. The FPC's exhaustive administrative findings, on everything from recreation to aesthetics, led to a decision to let the project go forward. That administrative oversight was unquestionably appropriate for infrastructure improvements to be built on public lands. Any such decision necessarily involves compromises between competing interests, which always leave someone disappointed no matter what the outcome. Yet thoroughness in review did not carry the day, because the opponents of the project pointed to some tardy evidence that might have had some influence on the outcome. The court fell to this temptation, and reopened the entire proceeding so that this evidence could be admitted. Why the administrative decision to follow stated hearing rules should be regarded as arbitrary and capricious was left unexplained.

The lesson, however, was quickly learned on both sides. *Scenic Hudson I* invites any organized opposition to sandbag the hearings by consciously holding in reserve some trivial testimony until the eleventh hour. It also invites administrators to delay hearings lest they be overturned for some trivial error if they decide to forge ahead. The combined effect of these two strategies makes delay inevitable and finality illusory. Justice delayed, moreover, quickly became justice denied when five years later the same court held, in *Scenic Hudson II,* that the FPC's earlier work was not "in vain," after a second thorough investigation supported the first. There are only two things wrong with this story. First, the decisions resulted in an unfortunate waste of time and expense in the first investigation. Second, the passage of time rendered the construction of the hydroelectric facility infeasible in part because of rising costs and the financial erosion of Consolidated Edison Company, and doubtless in part because of its new regulatory costs. Flouting procedures for short-term gain forms no part of the rule of law.

A similar story unfolded in *Citizens to Preserve Overton Park v. Volpe* (1971),[21] where the Supreme Court had to decide whether the U.S. secretary of transportation made a "feasible and prudent" decision in authorizing the use of federal funds for building a new six-lane interstate highway through Overton Park, in Memphis. Any decision on the use of public property requires an administrative proceeding, for which judicial deference seems sensible. Yet the Supreme Court chose instead to follow the "hard look" approach, which is better reserved for statutory interpretation where courts have real expertise. In particular, Justice Thurgood Marshall's opinion set an impossible standard for evaluating matters "committed to agency discretion by law" by insisting that these decisions rest only "on a consideration of the relevant factors," with a concurrent disregard of all irrelevant ones.[22] The endless permutations virtually ensure that some error will be made at the agency level, which is hardly a reason to begin the entire project again from scratch, only to repeat the process on appeal. Formality begets formality, which in turn begets delay—so much so, that this road, too, was never built.

In both of these cases, government officials, as *managers* of public projects, need more discretion in the conduct of their agencies than they receive when they act as *regulators* of private markets. No private collectivity that manages a museum, a corporation, or a real estate subdivision uses internal rules that allow it to act only with the consent of its most recalcitrant member. The same tough-minded attitude is required for the construction of social infrastructure needed to support the operations of the private market, which otherwise will shrivel and die.

The same attitude, moreover, carries over to fact-dense administrative determinations on health and safety, including many difficult decisions on automobile safety made pursuant to the National Traffic and Motor Vehicle Safety Act.[23] Many of the agency's actions are probably misplaced, given that overall levels of automobile safety appear to be driven by technology, not by the articulation of new legal standards. But even those critical of the act's role in ensuring safety must worry less about its repeal and more about its efficient operation. Measured against these concerns, the "hard look" doctrine fails. At first blush, judicial oversight of factual determinations by administrative agencies looks like a welcome assertion of judicial power over administrative action. All too often, however, it is used to extend, not restrict, the reach of the regulatory state.

Motor Vehicle Manufacturers' Association v. State Farm Mutual Automobile Insurance Co. (1983)[24] offers another illustration of how judicial overreaching in technical matters flies in the face of the sensible division between questions of fact and matters of law. Like the *Chevron* case, *State Farm* crystallized a conflict between the Carter and Reagan administrations, now over the use of passive restraints in automobiles. The Carter administration wanted to phase in passive-restraint devices, without testing alternative new devices, prior to 1982. The Reagan administration, however, overturned that decision in response to a blizzard of technical objections from the automobile industry. Justice Stevens found that the Reagan administration had acted in an arbitrary and capricious fashion for failing to consider whether to mandate untested airbags. Stevens's reckless and unconventional approach shows that his true motivation was to force-feed airbag safety deployment before its time. It was no coincidence that Stevens's ire was directed toward *deregulation.* New regulation would have been allowed under a far lower threshold.

So the inversion of modern judicial oversight of regulation is complete. Judicial abstinence now applies to questions of legal interpretation, while the same courts invoked the "arbitrary and capricious" standard to block new development in *Scenic Hudson* and *Citizens to Preserve Overton Park,* and to prevent deregulation in *State Farm.* Both deviations from the text of the Administrative Procedure Act pull us further away from the rule of law. Nor are they the only pressures. The specter of retroactive legislation has the same effect.

12

Retroactivity

The Faltering Constitutional Presumption against Retroactive Laws

Retroactive legislation poses yet another challenge to the rule of law. Such laws are routinely denounced under classical liberal theories because of their interference with settled expectations on which private citizens have a right to rely. Indeed, within that intellectual framework, there is little if any need to pass those laws in the first place. The basic framework of property, contract, and tort law is stable over a wide range of social circumstances. The need to adapt these systems to new technologies can usually be done by a simple extension of standard principles, without upsetting the previous set of rules.[1] For example, it is often said that the rise of intellectual-property law requires major changes in the fabric of ordinary property laws. But in fact, this proposition is false. The key difference between some forms of intellectual property—chiefly copyrights and patents—is that they need not last, and indeed under the United States Constitution cannot last, for unlimited periods of time.[2] Otherwise, the general sets of principles carry over from real estate to other forms of property. The rules on infringement follow from the rules of trespass. The general preference for injunctions over damages when both are possible follows from the same presumption that is used in cases of trespass (including permanent encroachment on the lands of others) and nuisance. The rules governing sales and licenses follow from the usual rules governing total and partial disposition of property. The use of special gimmicks could easily generate demands for retroactive laws, which a wiser system would put to one side. In similar fashion, the relatively simple flat tax of the classical liberal system is resistant to changes in fads or circumstances, and thus avoids the inevitable demand for technical corrections or revisions that arise when the tax code is replete with ad hoc compromises that lead to short-term solutions. It is no source of comfort that the current tax code, as a result of the great compromise in the lame-duck Congress in 2010, contains about 141 short-term tax code provisions, all of which are subject to renegotiation in ways that can easily invite retroactive changes.

In dealing with these issues, the conventional view was that retroactive laws were simply off-limits. That judgment is reflected in the U.S. Constitution, yet with the caveat that its prohibition applies only to retroactive criminal laws.[3] Under the Ex Post Facto Clause, states, for example, cannot simply suspend the statute of limitations against criminal prosecution for child abuse.[4] In the nineteenth century, the Supreme Court also held that the Contracts Clause afforded protection against various forms of debtor relief with respect to preexisting debts.[5] But today, the protections against retroactive imposition of liability are far weaker. One conspicuous illustration concerns the suspension of the statute of limitations, which now may be waived or suspended to allow for child abuse tort actions to be brought against the overseers or supervisors of the molesters, often in religious settings. In general, a watered-down version of the rational-basis test is used to reinstate the cause of action against the earlier concern with the preservation of settled expectations.[6] The judicial adherence to this standard holds firm even in the most dangerous situation, when a government agency acts as a plaintiff in litigation to offload its own expenses against private parties. Just that happens when the legislature suspends the operation of a statute of limitation in order to make it possible for the state to revive what would otherwise be the government's time-barred claim.[7] The risk of bias and self-interest should be obvious. The key question, then, is whether legislative efforts to undermine statutes of limitations should not be blocked by the two Due Process Clauses, one of which runs against the federal government and the other against the state governments. The due-process guarantee provides that no person should be deprived of life, liberty, or property without due process of law, yet it has almost uniformly failed to block any retroactive change in law that carries only civil penalties or liabilities. One shot at the apple should be enough.

Private Reliance and Government Expertise

Modern law is equally unwilling to set up firm guarantees against retroactive actions undertaken by administrative agencies. Yet routinely, most modern judges and scholars think that retroactive laws that expand the scope of administrative action in civil matters should pass constitutional muster. Here is their virtuous story. Everyone knows, of course, that complex administrative schemes can easily go awry. Necessarily, a retroactivity norm imposes significant restrictions on the ability of virtuous legislators to make midstream corrections to these large schemes. Knock down the retroactivity constraint, and legislators can better update a complex statutory regime based on information acquired after the passage or implementation of the act. Administrative neutrality and expertise again drive the basic norm.

The flip-side of the issue looks at the parallel dislocations imposed on private parties. Without a strong prohibition on retroactive legislation, there is never a time at which a private party can treat past transactions as closed. The greater latitude for legislative adjustments is thus offset by the higher costs of running private businesses that are vulnerable to these nonstop political maneuvers. The costs here are not trivial. Financing new ventures is made trickier whenever the government can impose by fiat an undisclosed lien on current and future assets. Firms that might otherwise remain in business might liquidate in advance to stave off new potential liabilities. New businesses may remain stillborn because their prospective owners fear being trapped once new legislation changes the rules of the game.

How then to compare the two types of risk? In principle, the simplest way to do this is by express contract. When the government desires flexibility in contracting with private parties, it can announce its position in advance, thereby letting private parties opt out. To be sure, governments usually act by legislation, not by contract. Yet here, too, the presumption should be against retroactive reversal of position, at least after reliance by the private party when it is no longer possible to return to the status quo ante. If the government does not like that position, let it reserve its option explicitly by legislation. After all, the two sides do not start from a position of parity. The state, as the dominant party, determines the rules of the game. It therefore should be under the burden to declare its option at the outset, if it wants to reserve the right to change the rules in the middle of the game. Right now, however, government silently casts the risk of retroactive change on private parties, who cut back on their activities accordingly. Indeed, the situation is even worse at present, for right now no private party can rely even on an explicit state promise not to change the laws. The current Supreme Court decisions on workers' compensation laws and mortgage and pension laws tell the same tale.

The Black Lung Benefits Act of 1972,[8] for example, required mine operators to fund compensation programs for pneumoconiosis, or black-lung disease, for both retired and active workers who had suffered from their employment in coal mines. The compensation programs were to be funded not out of general revenues, but solely by taxes levied exclusively on the operators who had employed those workers years before, without facing, under the applicable law of the time, any exposure to liability for black-lung disease. The pre-1937 Supreme Court cases had rejected any special retroactive liability scheme intended to fund private railroad retirement plans.[9] By analogy to such precedent, the retroactive black-lung compensation tax would seem to be unconstitutional, for the prohibition against retroactive rules applies to all closed obligations regardless of whether the barred claim arose from contractual or tort obligations.

But Justice Thurgood Marshall, in *Usery v. Turner Elkhorn Mining Co.* (1976),[10] sustained the tax, with a decision that landed like a bolt from the blue. "[O]ur cases are clear that legislation readjusting rights and burdens is not unlawful solely because it upsets otherwise settled expectations. This is true even though the effect of the legislation is to impose a new duty or liability based on past acts."[11] To Justice Marshall, this retroactive special tax counted "as a rational measure to spread the costs of the employees' disabilities to those who have profited from the fruits of their labor: the operators and the coal consumers," without any evidence that they had made any supracompetitive profits from their past activities.[12] Nor was the Supreme Court troubled that new entrants into the mining business were not saddled with similar charges. "[L]egislative Acts adjusting the burdens and benefits of economic life come to the Court with a presumption of constitutionality, and . . . the burden is on one complaining of a due process violation to establish that the legislature has acted in an arbitrary and irrational way."[13] *Turner Elkhorn* thus lets the legislature make liability rules as indefinite as modern property rights. Yet the same wasteful political competition takes place whether people are seeking to obtain legislative benefits or to avoid liability.

These ad hoc adjustments always breed further uncertainties. Predictably, the competitive imbalance in the mining industry led Congress to impose the special tax on new mining firms that had never benefited from the earlier practices. Next, the Supreme Court made a wobbly effort to cut back on the free-for-all in dumping liabilities in *Eastern Enterprises v. Apfel* (1998),[14] on the grounds that, unlike *Turner Elkorn,* the Coal Industry Retiree Health Benefit Act required firms to fund health care benefits for its former employees, now retired, who had worked for them before they had left the coal-mining industries. Why a subsequent shift in business plans could make retroactive liabilities more unacceptable was left unexplained. Yet rather than leading to a gradual erosion of *Turner Elkhorn, Eastern Enterprises* proved to have no staying power at all, as judges' acceptance of retroactive legislation remained undiminished.[15] The constitutional villain in these cases is once again the rational-basis test, which treats any bad argument as a good argument so long as it discharges at least one useful social objective. In practice, retroactive legislation always passes muster under that test. For example, the retroactive black-lung tax passed because the new legal regime conferred benefits on some miners who were part of the winning political coalition. The imposition of any industry-specific tax will also cause profound dislocations. But so long as political actors are not prepared to pay for these benefits out of general revenues, the economic uncertainty will remain. And so the precarious nature of legal assets and legal liabilities leads to a reduction in overall investment levels by individuals who are unwilling to bear the political risks.

A similar level of legal instability arises when the government retroactively alters financial obligations. The Supreme Court's Depression-era case of *Home Building & Loan v. Blaisdell* (1934)[16] upheld a mortgage moratoria program that forced lenders to postpone the collection of their loans. In principle, these devices should be acceptable if the renegotiated loan gives the lender sufficient security to cover the risks of delay. But in the ordinary two-party situation, that result could be worked out between the parties voluntarily. Therefore, the need for the forced stay of execution typically arises only in those bankruptcy cases in which it is necessary to keep some specific asset that is essential for preserving the "ongoing value" of a firm that is going into reorganization, a task that is not easy to accomplish. But the situation in the 1930s had an added element of complexity because persistent deflation required that loans be repaid with more expensive dollars than those that had been borrowed. That defect, however, can be countered only if one keeps faith with yet another cardinal principle from the classical liberal play-book: the preservation of a stable unit of public currency, which can serve as a reliable ruler for all private transactions. Unfortunately, no adjustment of the risk of default between lender and borrower can neu-tralize this deflationary mistake.

The flawed logic of *Blaisdell*, however, extended to cases in which there was no risk of currency fluctuation. Thus, the Supreme Court let the United States force individual firms to pay penalties on withdrawing from the Pension Benefit Guaranty Fund, notwithstanding the govern-ment's explicit earlier contractual promise that withdrawal was permis-sible, without penalty, at any time.[17] "Prudent employers then had more than sufficient notice not only that pension plans were currently regu-lated, but also that withdrawal itself might trigger additional financial obligations."[18] This logic turns classical liberal theory on its head. The strongest reason for protection against retroactive liability lies in the sure knowledge that governments left to their own devices will revise or nullify their covenants to escape financial responsibility for their own mistakes. The general awareness of that tendency was the reason for im-posing the safeguard, not the reason for disregarding it. Notice of the risk of default is there in every case, and the right question to ask is whether the party who received notice has agreed to take the risk or has in fact used that notice as the reason for negotiating higher levels of protection against the identified risk. Just showing that a party has no-tice does not begin to answer the question of whether it took the risk of the misconduct of which it was all too aware.

These bad decisions have long-term consequences to this day. Since the subprime meltdown of 2007, mortgage markets have been roiled by bad practices generating excessive loans on insufficient security, many of which tanked when the real estate market failed. Unrelenting political pressures led to requirements that lenders postpone collection or otherwise renegotiate their loans. In many cases, prudent lenders might make that choice in any event. But allowing government officials to substitute their own judgments for those of the lenders whose money is at stake is asking for trouble. The private renegotiation will take place only when the lender's best guess is that the net losses from foreclosure are greater than those from renegotiation. Government pandering to political interests, by contrast, works from a different calculus, with worse results. The government moratoria that postponed the default did not cure the underlying problems with the debtor. Foreclosure comes, if at all, only after further deterioration in property values. The unwillingness to book these economic losses immediately also delays the resale of the property at prices that reflect the diminished market value of the underlying property. The thin markets have in turn made it more difficult for the holders of securitized interests to value or rationalize their frayed portfolios. The markets thus remain in an economic disequilibrium that prevents the repricing of assets that would allow for rapid trade, albeit at lower prices.

Finally, the fear of similar government strategies in the future saps lenders' confidence that their new loans will be protected, and this concern leads them to hedge their bets in the housing markets. Once again, the instability of property rights in a regime of retroactive invalidation of market transactions shows that the rule of law cannot survive in a regime of weak property rights, at least not in a constitutional regime that applies a weak rational-basis review to all property transactions. Stable substantive and procedural rules are both needed to counteract the risk that unfettered political discretion will undermine voluntary transactions. Yet those characteristics are impossible in the administrative state that denigrates fixed rules and exalts government discretion. There is no necessary reason that an administrative state cannot be compatible with the rule of law. But empirically, the only way in which it can operate is to violate or ignore the components of the rule of law that Lon Fuller recognized two generations ago.

13

Modern Applications:
Financial Reform
and Health Care

The previous chapters showed how the extension of the administrative power of the state has placed greater pressure on the procedural values associated with the rule of law. These vices are all-too-present in the two major legislative achievements of the first two years of the Obama administration, the Dodd-Frank Wall Street Reform and Consumer Protection Act of 2010 (Dodd-Frank Act),[1] and the Patient Protection and Affordable Care Act (ACA),[2] which reshapes the provision of health care in the United States. Both of these statutes represent a level of regulatory ambition that far exceeds in scope and complexity any New Deal regulation of financial markets. No short book can summarize Dodd-Frank, a statute that requires, depending on how the count is carried out, between 240 and 540 new rule-making procedures,[3] or the ACA, which represents the same level of obscurity. But it is easy to demonstrate that the high levels of regulatory ambition have led to a corresponding reduction in the standard level of protections associated with the rule of law mentioned earlier. I will start with Dodd-Frank and then turn to the ACA.

The Dodd-Frank Act

One notable institutional innovation of Dodd-Frank is the creation of the Financial Stability Oversight Council (FSOC),[4] charged with the oversight of the entire financial system of the United States—oversight extending not only to the large banks, but also to a bewildering variety of nonbank financial institutions—insurance companies and hedge funds, for example—that are said in some way to pose a "systematic risk" to the soundness of the overall banking system. The goal is to make sure that no single institution is "too big to fail," and that no government funds will have to be committed to future bailouts.[5] One possible way to achieve much of these objectives is to commit in advance to a no-bailout policy of the sort that was used selectively to save the AIG insurance corporation, but not Lehman Brothers, from oblivion. But in this instance, exactly the opposite course was plotted, as the FSOC gets involved full scale in all these operations.

The evident risk for bias in this operation starts with the question of what sizes of institutions are included in this scheme, and why. In dealing with banks, Dodd-Frank establishes a threshold of $50 billion in assets; any bank of this size rates an automatic inclusion. Clearly, some line has to be drawn, and to many unpracticed eyes, $50 billion in assets seems like a large number. But a little bit of perspective is needed, insofar as the three largest banks are Bank of America, at $2.3 trillion, and J. P. Morgan Chase and Citibank, at about $2 trillion each. There is thus a forty-fold size difference between the largest and smallest covered entities, which raises the simple question of how any failure at the low end of this distribution can have that effect at all.

The situation only gets more tenuous because the list of covered institutions also contains those firms, or classes of firms, that the FSOC deems suitable for oversight function. Here, the difference between inclusion and exclusion has tremendous ramifications, given the huge level of oversight on routine business transactions prior to any systematic failure, such that the FSOC "may provide for more stringent regulation of a financial activity . . . or practice conducted by bank holding companies or nonbank financial companies."[6] Long before any risk of failure, coverage under Dodd-Frank is so exhaustive that the statute should be regarded as a potential first step toward the nationalization of all the large and diverse financial institutions brought within its scope. That question of coverage, moreover, is not one that will proceed in a disinterested fashion in which technical considerations will dominate. Once the status of a bank or financial institution matters this much, constant efforts will be made by private parties to stay outside the FSOC's orbit, and, of course, to explain in ever-so-prudent terms why it is that some competitive industry or firm in reality needs to be subject to regulation that should never in a thousand Sundays be applied to the supplicant institution. Discretion this broad is not without its antecedent consequences.

Once it becomes clear who is covered, and why, the next task is to develop criteria to figure out what should be done. Once again, the decision has to be made early in the market cycle, in anticipation of a potential meltdown. The situation thus contrasts with normal bankruptcy proceedings, which are brought into play only much later in the cycle of financial decline, when greater information is available about the financial conditions of the particular firm and about the broader market context in which that firm operates. That more modest mission is one reason ordinary bankruptcy courts, if left free of political pressure, could do a better job of winding up a complex company in rational fashion. But Dodd-Frank does not rely on using the prospect of reorganization or liquidation in bankruptcy as a way to incentivize large firms to stay out of trouble. Rather, it takes on that task itself, and must perforce rely on a set of generous and open-ended criteria that are easy to state and difficult to apply. At this point, the scheme deviates from the traditional courts of law in two ways. First, it does not operate by "known and indifferent" judges, but entrusts the burden of decisionmaking in individual cases to a group of stressed-out individuals, each of whom has extensive management obligations over some segment of the United States financial system.

More concretely, the FSOC is composed of various agency heads of government, which include the heads of the Securities and Exchange Commission, the Commodities Futures Trading Commission, the Federal Housing Finance Agency, the Office of the Comptroller of Currency, the Federal Deposit Insurance Corporation, the Bureau of Financial Consumer Protection, the Federal Reserve Board, the National Credit Union Administration Board, and one lone individual with expertise in insurance. The operation is headed by the secretary of the Treasury, who is given extra powers under the law, for none of the FSOC's powers can be exercised over his opposition. He must be in the two-thirds majority of people who either force some financial institution into the oversight of the Federal Reserve or remove that oversight.

The most obvious feature about this list is that it includes individuals whose major responsibilities in other areas invite a clash of wills with the very institutions that run the risk of being thrown into government receivership by these collective actions. The web of influence is impossible to predict in advance. Indeed, it may well be impossible to follow once these programs are implemented. But as with all cases of bias, the inability to track the diffuse and subtle forms of causal influence has led to the maxim that not only should bias be avoided, but it should be *seen* to be avoided as well. In this labyrinth, that goal is impossible to achieve. The connections are too deeply embedded in the DNA of these multiple, fractious, and overlapping government agencies.

The dangers of government overreach are only compounded by the prolix criteria that are everywhere invoked to decide whether—and if so, how—a private institution will be brought into government orbit. For example, the definition of a "nonbank financial institution" is far from clear, but covers companies both domestic and foreign that are "predominantly engaged in, including through a branch in the United States, financial activities, as defined in paragraph (6)."[7] Yet that paragraph provides no lifeline when it states that a firm predominantly so behaves so long as 85 percent of its assets are "financial in nature." At this point, the next question requires the FSOC to determine whether a particular company is in "material financial distress," or that its "nature, scope, size, scale concentration, interconnectedness, or mix of activities" are such that the firm—either alone or in combination, one assumes— "could pose a threat to the financial stability of the United States."[8] Rules of this sort do not admit of clear lines, to say the least, and unlike the common-law rules that relied on reasonableness determinations to fill in gaps in a larger system (see Chapter 3), there are no permanent structural features that inform the exercise of discretion. At best, there is a laundry list of factors relating to leverage (i.e., equity-to-debt ratios, which are not easy to calculate when there are multiple tiers of capital), off-balance-sheet financing, and a meta-factor which includes "any other risk-related factors that the [FSOC] deems appropriate"—which is to say, any factor at all. The degrees of freedom that are allowed to this body are sufficiently great that it would be hard to find any decision that counts as right or wrong at all.

There is an open question, under American constitutional law, whether delegated authority of this extent is an impermissible hand-off of legislative power to an unelected administrative body. As a historical matter, there have been only two cases, *Panama Refining v. Ryan*[9] and *A.L.A. Schechter Poultry v. United States*[10] (both decided in 1935), which struck down statutes on the grounds that they conferred excessive delegation on administrative agencies.

Panama Refining was concerned with setting the appropriate prices for "hot oil" (i.e., oil shipped improperly across state lines) in a market that experienced dramatic price movements because of the uncertain supply of oil. *Schechter* involved the setting of wages and prices, and the rules for the purchase of "sick" chickens under the National Industrial Recovery Act of 1933. In both cases, the rules of engagement for a single industry were involved. In each case, the agency promulgated general rules that, however unwise, were knowable in advance. It is a brave lawyer who would rely on these two decisions in attacking Dodd-Frank, as these cases have not survived the test of time. Within a decade, the Supreme Court sustained an entire system of wartime price controls under the Office of Price Administration, governed by a general standard of equitable conduct that starts with historical prices and then works forward.[11]

The difficulty in this case is coterminous with the ambition of the government problem. No sane person can think that a command which orders an administrator to "in his judgment . . . be generally fair and equitable and . . . effectuate the purposes of this Act" in those circumstances where, in the judgment of the administrator, prices "have risen or threaten to rise to an extent or in a manner inconsistent with the purposes of this Act," is as clear as a command that orders a fine for driving in excess of 60 miles per hour. Yet so long as there is a political will to impose a regime of price controls, whether in wartime or in peacetime, statutes with this level of generality will be upheld because it is impossible for any court to draft a statute that is consistent with the scope of the enterprise and that has clearer language. The difficulty, quite simply, is this: only vague language can launch the enterprise, so that all parties caught in the web will never be able to challenge its validity. The most they can ask for is an administrative determination that upholds or denies the order in ways that give the party a chance to comply. The requisite notice comes not from the statute but from the particular commands made pursuant to it.

This system works, after a fashion, for price controls, but it is an open question whether it can be applied in anything other than a rubber-stamp way with respect to the complex commands that Dodd-Frank allows the FSOC to impose on the bank and nonbank institutions that fall under its thumb. As one might expect, the vastness of the delegated authority carries with it a truncated set of judicial procedures that may be used to challenge any order under it. In good Kafkaesque fashion, the abbreviated procedures for nonbank organizations require written notice of the proposed actions of the FSOC, after which the firm is allowed thirty days in which to request a written or oral hearing to present its views to a body that, having already made up its mind, is now allowed to hear what the other side has to say. Even these slender protections can be shortened to ten days by the same two-thirds vote for an "emergency exception."[12] Oral hearings matter, for they force judges to put themselves on the record or to be embarrassed by their silence. The mail order sanctions, in a manner of this sort, do not seem to meet the most elementary considerations of due process.

The situation is no better when it comes to judicial review, which the statute allows within a thirty-day period. But the scope of the review "shall be limited to whether the final determination made under this section was arbitrary and capricious,"[13] where that standard does not invite the kind of "hard look" that was applied to the judicial review of the *State Farm* decision making safety interlock devices optional;[14] rather, the decision is subject to a highly forgiving standard that resembles rational-basis review. No effort to challenge the constitutionality of the statute or even an interpretation of its basic provision is allowed within the judicial setting.

So long as judicial review appears to require some degree of oversight on administrative tribunals that have strong vested interests, this procedure seems presumptively to fail. The only justification is that great speed is needed to deal with matters of huge financial import. Yet oddly enough for many of these actions, even a day, not to mention a month, is enough for a downward cycle to play itself out, so that, ironically, the supposedly speedy review may well turn out to be far too slow to allow for effective intervention. At this point, more regular procedures seem indicated. For those great emergencies, the entire effort to coerce compliance, especially with smaller entities, looks to be a misguided venture from the get-go. The sensible thing is to engage in short-term activities that prop up a business with federal funds, rather than to drive it into bankruptcy though an excessive set of regulations which will never be challenged as a taking of private property, even if the government actions drive a firm over the edge. Yet the ability to open the spigot, whether wise or foolish, still remains, which only makes more insistent the question of what point this entire operation can serve. The moral of the story seems to ring true. The excessive ambition of regulation is ill thought-out to begin with. But from that point on, the basic maxim holds. Bloated government missions can go forward only if the most rudimentary protections of the rule of law are systematically pushed to one side.

The Patient Protection and Affordable Care Act

A similar set of objections should also be lodged against the vast extension of federal power under the 2010 Patient Protection and Affordable Care Act (ACA).[15] The ACA confers on both the federal government and the states vast new powers to regulate all aspects of the health care industry. Virtually all of the powers so conferred under the ACA are flatly contrary to the vision of the rule of law that I have set forth throughout this book.

As a general matter of political theory, there are two ways in which to attack a health care system which everyone agrees is broken. The first is to look for those systems of regulation that impede the ordinary operation of market forces and then repeal them.[16] The list of such impediments is long, and growing, and includes licensing restrictions that prevent doctors from moving between states, licensing restrictions that prevent businesses from setting up health care practices that rely more heavily on technology and nonphysician personnel to handle cases, restrictions on the sale of insurance across state lines, insurance mandates that allow the purchase of insurance by employers only if certain coverages are included, and so on down the line. Their repeal costs nothing to administer, except for a few modest transition provisions.

Reducing overall costs also increases access to the private market, which in turn reduces the number of uninsureds—a group that has grown inexorably in the past thirty years under current policies. The economic downturn in the past three years resulted in a deterioration of the overall health care system, with the following highlights.[17] People without any health care insurance: *up* to 16.7 percent in 2009, from 15.4 percent in 2008. People with health insurance: *down* to 253.6 million in 2009, from 255.1 million in 2008. People with private health care insurance: *down* to 194.5 million in 2009, from 201 million in 2008, for a decline of covered individuals from 66.7 percent to 63.9 percent. People covered by employer health care plans: *down* to 169.7 million people in 2009, from 176.3 million people in 2008, for a decline of persons covered by their employer to 55.8 percent in 2009 from 58.5 percent in 2008, representing the lowest level since these statistics were first recorded in 1987. In contrast, people with government health insurance: *up* to 93.2 million in 2009, from 87.4 million in 2008. The numbers speak of a slow implosion of the entire market.

The question now is what accounts for this shift. On the private side, the best answer is: high unemployment rates coupled with exacting mandates and conditions that must be satisfied if these plans are to continue to operate. The great fear here is that the impact of the ACA will only exacerbate these risks. The high levels of uncertainty in labor markets will continue to drive firms to prefer to hire temporary employees in order to avoid the costly mandates. The new mandates will force prices up, so that many employers will drop or reduce coverage for their existing employees.

It is impossible here to go through all the complex factors that drive this analysis, but we can isolate two illustrative portions of the statute that make it likely that the high levels of discretion in the hands of public officials will lead to a major contraction of the private sector, and perhaps to its elimination. The first deals with the well-known individual mandate that requires all individuals to maintain "minimum essential coverage" by making—in communitarian newspeak—a "shared responsibility payment" by way of penalty for failing to keep private coverage in place; the payment is set at $2,000, subject to a complex set of limitations and adjustments.[18] The second is the system of quasi–price fixing that is imposed for those private companies that wish to sell their services on the state-run "exchange" systems through which low-income individuals can purchase health care insurance with the benefit of a hefty government subsidy. Let me take these in order.

THE INDIVIDUAL MANDATE. The obvious criticism of the individual mandate is that the government imposes a penalty on individuals, even though they have done no wrong. In effect, it is as though the government has sought to conscript individuals who wish to mind their own business into the service of a larger social cause in which they would rather not participate. There are two common justifications for these mandated payments. The first is to prevent the rise of individual free riders who will stay out of the system when healthy, only to join it opportunistically when the need arises. The second is to fund the extensive obligations to those individuals who are granted access to the system as of right, notwithstanding their greater health risks or preexisting conditions. The object here is not to canvass the constitutional cases, but to show that the necessary somersaults in public administration will both compromise interests in private property and undermine the rule of law.

As a matter of public outcry, the individual mandate is without question the most unpopular of the provisions of the ACA.[19] The command is easily understood, and is widely resented for its authoritarian implications. The issue in these cases is often raised obliquely in connection with the scope of federal power under the Commerce Clause, which says: "Congress shall have the power . . . to regulate . . . commerce among the several states."[20] The argument here is that the broad modern construction of the idea of commerce still does not comprehend the ability to force people into commerce against their will, even if it allows Congress broad powers to regulate those who choose to enter commercial relations, including farmers who use their own wheat to feed their own cows.[21] That argument was accepted in at least one fed-

eral case.[22] But an odd point about this argument is that it takes a concern that is related to individual autonomy and uses it to deal with matters of federal power rather than with ordinary questions of individual
liberty. The issues of state commandeering would be every bit as large,
or small, if an individual state imposed this kind of a mandate on its
citizens. Individual autonomy is a key value against both state and national governments.

Looked at in that way, the government's free-rider argument shows
how easy it is to take the sensible concern with public goods and twist it
into an unrecognizable form. The standard public good is a street light
or a defense system. The light must provide illumination to all, whether
they pay for it or not. The defense shield covers all, whether they pay for
it or not. The customary argument for the voluntary provision of these
services thus fails for nonexcludable goods, for, absent organized state
coercion, each rational and self-interested (as opposed to civic-minded)
individual will be happily willing to let others pay for the benefit that he
can consume with them on equal terms.[23] The tax system thus forces
each person to pay for a good that all people desire but which they could
not obtain by voluntary means themselves. The basic argument is that
public financing of public goods thus gives to each person a gain larger
than the tax that he or she incurs. Ideally, these taxes are imposed only
in those situations, and at those levels, that generate Pareto improvements. Indeed, as noted earlier, the political system will be more stable
if these gains are roughly pro rata for all individuals. There is no need to
secure redistribution among private individuals in order to overcome
the chronic problem of the underprovision of public goods in voluntary
markets.

The health care mandate has nothing whatsoever to do with free
riders and public goods. Health care is a private good because medical
care for one can be provided without supplying it on equal terms to all.
The great virtue of a market is that it allows insurance companies before
the fact to set rates that have two desirable characteristics. The companies can make money by issuing insurance coverage to a large pool of

individuals, so long as the expected payouts under the plan are less than the revenues it receives. The law of large numbers, with a dose of reinsurance, allows every individual to diversify risk. On the other side, each individual wants to stay in the pool regardless of who else is in it, because the benefits all people receive exceed the premium costs. There are gains from trade to both parties, and no efforts at redistribution that create the need to manage cross-subsidies.

This system can founder in practice if individuals who have a great need for health care cannot afford the premiums needed to get protection. At this point, the clear sense that individual wealth and individual need are weakly correlated can lead to public, as well as private, responses. One question is whether these individuals should receive aid, and if so, how much. But once any assistance is required, the key funding question is how to cover the costs that no market can supply. In earlier days, charitable institutions, coupled with reduced physician fees in cases of need, covered most of the shortfall. Today, the large-government solution is to tax some in order to provide for others. The case for redistribution is, as noted earlier, always tenuous, but within limits it has great appeal (which is why charitable institutions work as a voluntary matter in the first place). But at no point is free riding ever an issue.

The real question is one of technique. Under the ACA, private insurance is so regulated that individuals no longer pay a premium that reflects their expected costs to the system. By explicit command, the spreads between the young and the old, for example, are shrunk so as to provide a subsidy for the old. When young people flee the system, they do so to avoid a subsidy, which hardly makes them free riders. The government ignores this effort to escape cross-subsidy only to stress another. It notes that public facilities are kept open to all people in need, regardless of their ability to pay. Yet any "free riding" here can be cured in either of two ways. First, simply deny open access to those who do not pay or acquire insurance for just that purpose, which is unlikely to cost the fee levied by the individual health care mandate, most of which will probably fund the cross-subsidy.[24] Second, fund the open-access system with general public revenues, which are explicit costs that can then be taken into account in a clear and open way. What cannot be done is to pretend that individuals are free riders because they refuse to pay government subsidies or because they take advantage of free services that the government could revoke at any time. To allow the free-rider argument here is to allow it in all cases in which government wishes to engage in massive forms of covert redistribution, which undermines the system of private property by effectively removing major constraints against state power. So long as health care involves goods that can be supplied to one but not the next, there is no public-goods problem. Nor is there any form of market failure, given the absence of any blockade of voluntary transactions. What is wanting is a lack of redistribution through a form of "social insurance," in which, as its advocates candidly admit, *the element of cross-subsidy is essential.*[25] But to call this a market failure means that every voluntary transaction that produces mutual gains to parties counts as a market failure, which then means that all markets are by definition "failures"—a truly untenable result.

MEDICAL LOSS RATIOS. A second major distortion of the health care system relates to the impossible pressures that the ACA places on all private providers of health care. Normal insurance markets work by allowing private insurers to decide whom they will insure, what they will insure their customer for, and how much they will charge. Competitive forces bring supply into line with demand, and lead all parties to acquire protection only against those risks that they select. Under this system, no insurer ever faces any mandate of the type which says that if it wishes to write coverage, it must accede to these conditions. Those mandates immediately invoke the problem of unconstitutional conditions (see Chapter 1), for they say, even though an employer or insurer need not supply insurance, if it does, that insurance must follow certain prescribed lines.

The market inefficiency in these cases is simple. If the item mandated is worth more than it costs, it will be supplied voluntarily. If not, it will not be supplied in a voluntary market. But once it is mandated, it will do one of two things. Either it will lead to a reduction in the net value of the coverage offered, which is equal to the sum of the consumer surplus and the producer surplus, where the first represents the value above cost of the policy to the consumer, and the second represents the value of the policy to the producer over the cost of its supply. The sum of the two is equal to the overall social value from the policy, and that number can decline when mandates are imposed, even when the employer decides to keep the policy in place. Alternatively, the mandates could lead the employer to drop the coverage. The former will occur when the gains from the remainder of the policy are greater than the losses associated with the mandated coverage. The latter will occur when that inequality is reversed, so that the coverage produces less than the loss incurred by the mandate. The more mandates that are added, the more likely it is that the coverage will fail. It is largely for this reason that mandates have driven down the number of employees who are covered in employer plans.

The difficulty with the ACA is that it wants to win both ways. It wants to extend coverage, yet also to sweeten the benefit packages simultaneously. It therefore contains extensive mandates that require particular types of plans to offer various types of services in ways specified by the officials in the Department of Health and Human Services (HHS). The list covers the duty to insure preexisting conditions,[26] guaranteed renewal of insurance coverage,[27] and fair health insurance premiums, which limits the variation in insurance rates by age to a three-to-one ratio, and thus in practice requires younger insureds to subsidize older ones.[28] But those costs will raise prices, which will drive people out of the market.

To forestall that unfortunate outcome, the ACA introduces an extensive set of government subsidies to low-income individuals who purchase coverage on government "American Health Benefit Exchanges,"[29] which are open only to those qualified health plans that meet an elaborate set of government requirements intended to make them both accessible and efficient.[30] The entire scheme is overseen by HHS, which has the obligation to make sure that these exchanges generate sufficient choices so as to be user-friendly to persons with "significant health needs" or who are deemed "low-income, medically underserved individuals."[31]

This cornucopia also puts huge pressures on individual insurance companies to keep rates down. This is done not through a direct system of price controls, but through a set of close substitutes. One requirement is that these plans must "submit a justification for any premium increase" prior to its implementation. It is not as though HHS or the states can reject the increase, but they can exclude a firm from the exchanges, and the subsidies they supply, if the firm does not accept these terms. In addition, the ACA seeks to control health care costs through the so-called "medical loss ratio," which limits the "administrative costs" on large group insurance to 15 percent and those on small group or individual plans to 20 percent.[32] Those numbers are below the existing administrative costs currently associated with the operations of these plans, which run about 10 percent higher. The implicit justification for the ACA approach is that competition in private markets does not drive down costs, so that direct limitation on administrative costs becomes the proper hammer to force these costs lower. That outlook, unfortunately, encapsulates the same colossal blunder inherent in all systems of price and rent controls. It drives up the costs of doing business, but offers no rational way to reduce costs, which every firm has every incentive to do in any event. Instead, the provision leads to an orgy of administrative disputes as to what does and does not count as an administrative cost, which once again leads to the broad delegations of authority that stress public administration and lead to procedural shortcuts that undermine the rule of law.

The structure has no stable resting point, for something has to give when benefits are pushed up as rates are pushed down. And precisely that result is likely to happen when there are no constraints placed on the definition of the minimum elements of medical care that belong in the required bundles. There is little reason to expect any price resistance from low-income individuals who receive the largest subsidies from these plans. It is always easy to spend someone else's money, so that the government, as the payer for many of these expenses, has to find some way to price the bundles of services that are supplied, for which there is no obvious benchmark, given the huge regulatory pressures that the ACA exerts over the entire market. It is quite possible that the system could implode if the government mandates on the one side are not met by the government revenues on the other. In addition, some firms might well take the option to pay $2,000 per employee to be rid of obligations that will cost the government far more money to service. This double pincer movement between stiff price controls and inexorable service demands comes to resemble a system of public-utility regulation, whereby individual companies are required to supply certain costs for rates set by the government—without ensuring that the newly regulated companies earn a sufficient amount on their business capital to supply to future investors a rate of return sufficient to attract capital.[33]

Long before any constitutional challenge could materialize on this question, the federal government will be hard-pressed to let any major program go under because it cannot meet the required medical loss ratio. The point has special urgency before 2014, because no alternative program is now in place. So this process leads to a profound threat to the rule of law, by what I like to call "government by waiver." For example, the mini-med plans used for many low-wage employees have high administrative costs associated with the high turnover of workers —an element that government planners did not put into their rate calculations.[34] So McDonald's and other large employers threatened to drop coverage unless they receive a waiver from the medical loss waiver requirement, which was duly granted;[35] but this was followed by a directive from HHS that requires the operators of these plans to disclose the low level of benefits to their customers in plain language within sixty days of enrollment—as if that were not already known.[36] With or without notice, waiver is no way to run a government. These waivers are for one year only, and it is unclear whether or not they will be renewed. Administrative expenses can fluctuate from year to year, and the regulators may well have good reason to examine the books of an employer or to question its motivation. In light of the individual complexities, it is possible that these waivers will be offered to some individuals but not to others, and often the reasons for the distinction are not clear, to say the least. The entire system creates huge competitive distortions between those firms that get waivers and those that do not. Yet any form of judicial review challenging a denial of a waiver is likely to do too little and come too late. The high level of administrative discretion will make it hard to attack inconsistent judgments, for it is difficult to insist on the maxim "Treat like cases alike," when all firms occupy somewhat different market niches.

Yet in practice, there really is no way to escape this bind, once the statutory framework is laid down. Systems of positive rights have the modest virtue of curing small market failures by creating larger government failures. In so doing, they create huge pockets of government discretion which will spawn strategic behavior by the regulated firms and arbitrary behavior by the government officials that run the system. Yet there is no way to tweak the system and slow down this cycle born of distrust. Markets seek to reduce transaction costs to get higher levels of participation and greater amounts of consumer surplus. State regulation does the opposite. It raises transaction costs, increases the level of uncertainty, and opens the system up to constant levels of political intrigue in which stable expectations are hard to form. Right now, there are constitutional challenges to the various pieces of the ACA, and major efforts to secure its modification, postponement, or possible repeal. In light of the ACA's unpopularity, a Republican House could well seek to choke it off through withholding federal appropriations; states could refuse to cooperate in its implementation; individuals and employers can work nonstop games on the various rules for short-term private advantage. Yet none of this should be a surprise. The basic strength of a system of private property is that it reduces the play in the joints in the public sector, which in turn leads to controlled discretion and the real prospect of meeting the modest but critical aspirations of the rule of law.

In sum, these brief accounts of financial reform and health care reform illustrate the central proposition of this book. Ambitious social agendas introduce massive amounts of administrative discretion that are inconsistent with the rule of law.

14

Final Reflections

The purpose of this volume has been to pursue the interaction of three elements: private property, public administration, and the rule of law. Any viable legal system needs to have all three, and must therefore work out ways to distribute responsibilities between public and private actors. When it comes to making such choices, it is worth remembering that in most instances, private parties do not have anything approaching a monopoly position, and thus are at least somewhat constrained in how they behave by the presence of strong competitive forces. Governments have a monopoly of force within their jurisdictions, and thus are likely to face less discipline from market forces, even in a federalist system that affords citizens some protection by way of exit rights that allow them to vote with their feet. In dealing with these two sources of power, the trick is to try to leave the highest levels of discretion in the hands of those parties who are hemmed in by the strongest competitive forces. In general, therefore, the nod goes to private ordering.

That preference, however, can hardly be absolute in light of two risks. The first is the private use of force and fraud. The second is the abuse of monopoly power. It is to combat those behaviors that governments are instituted, so that they can use their own force to combat the dangers of any private system of control. Yet once they are endowed with that power, the question still remains: Who guards the guardians? That challenge cannot be answered by pointing to a group of Platonic guardians who stand outside the social order. Rather, such protection must come from a set of institutional arrangements that rely on the rule of law to constrain the behavior of public actors in two ways. First, the rule of law limits the areas in which public officials have discretion. Second, the rule of law helps incline public officials to use sound discretion in the exercise of their powers.

The rule of law as a bulwark against arbitrary power receives approbation. I can think of no working political figure or academic who disparages the importance of the rule of law, which, when all is said and done, is one welcome constraint against the exercise of arbitrary power. That principle had its inception in the earliest times, when the top-down power of monarchs was at its peak and where the rule of law served as a counterweight to the tyranny of a single individual. But it quickly spread to democratic societies, where the new risk was the tyranny of the majority. In and of itself, the rule-of-law principle does put important brakes on political power, but its effectiveness depends in large measure on the substantive legal regime with which it has to interact.

On this score, rules of property and contract fare well because the formulation of those substantive rights reinforces the traditional concerns of the rule of law on matters of clarity, consistency, simplicity, and prospectivity. The universal negative rights of forbearance are knowable, stable, and scalable, and independent of the particular levels of wealth in any society. The principles of contract require courts to enforce agreements made by others, and not to impose a set of ad hoc obligations whose content can be determined only through political processes. The great bane of the modern administrative state is its need to extend vast amounts of discretion to political actors who are subject to political forces that no abstract commitment to neutrality and expertise can overcome. Discretion is, to many people, the better part of valor. But not in public affairs, where discretion leads to the creation of indefinite property rights that invite political maneuvering of the types that traditionally have marred areas of labor and land use regulation. The recent domestic forays on matters of financial reform and health care have produced bloated and ill-conceived legislation that promises to bring out the worst in administrative excesses, so long as that legislation is on the books. The question remaining is whether passage of these laws represents a high point in the scope of government, from which the tides will ebb, or whether it represents a new plateau, from which retreat will be extremely difficult. The great power shifts that took place in Congress at the 2010 midterm elections have not resolved this issue. They could signal a real change of collective will on the matter. Or they could simply indicate a change in the winds of political fortune, in which political favors will be conferred on a different class of undeserved beneficiaries. Only time will tell.

Older writings used to say that the system of private property abhors a vacuum. This meant that once politics is allowed to fill in the gaps, huge amounts of energy that should be directed toward productive activities will be turned to the grim task of seeing how to take advantage of the political vulnerabilities of others. Every society has to suffer that drag to some degree. But once those forces are unleashed and celebrated, it is only a question of time as to how long a political order can prosper. Historically, we witness a constant battle between the forces of science and technology that expand the social pie, and the forces of faction and politics that eat away at those gains. Once upon a time, I was confident that the forces of growth and prosperity could maintain the upper hand. But watching the flailing of political actors, and the drift of our economic system, I am no longer so sure.

Notes

Indexes

Notes

Introduction

1. Woodrow Wilson, *Congressional Government: A Study in American Politics* (1885).

2. Federal Trade Commission Act of 1914, Pub. L. No. 63-203, 38 Stat. 717 (1914) (codified as amended in 15 U.S.C. §§41–58 [2006]).

3. Pub. L. 63-212, 38 Stat. 730 (1914) (codified as amended in 15 U.S.C. §§12–27 [2002]).

4. 26 Stat. 209 (1890) (codified as amended in 15 USC §§1–7 [2004]).

5. Tariff Act of 1930 (Smoot-Hawley Tariff), Pub. L. No. 71-361, 46 Stat. 590 (codified as amended at 19 U.S.C. §§1202–1677k [2006]).

6. Pub. L. No. 71-798, 46 Stat. 1494 (1931) (codified as amended at 40 U.S.C. §§3141–3148 [2006]).

7. Pub. L. No. 72-154, 47 Stat. 169 (1932).

8. Pub. L. No. 72-65, 47 Stat. 70 (1932) (codified as amended at 29 U.S.C. §102 [2006]).

9. 49 Stat. 449 (1935) (codified as amended at 29 U.S.C. §§151–169 [2006]).

10. Pub. L. No. 73-10, 48 Stat. 31 (1933) (codified as amended at 7 U.S.C. §§601–624 [2006]).

11. Securities and Exchange Act of 1934, Pub. L. No. 73-291, 48 Stat. 881 (codified as amended at 15 U.S.C. §§78d [2002]).

12. Pub. L. No. 75-718, 52 Stat. 1060 (1938) (codified as amended at 29 U.S.C. §§201–219 [2006]).

13. Social Security Act of 1935, Pub. L. No. 74-271, 49 Stat. 620 (codified as amended in scattered sections of 42 U.S.C.).

14. Pub. L. No. 88-452, 78 Stat. 508, 42 U.S.C. §2701 (repealed 1981).

15. Pub. L. No. 88-352, 78 Stat. 241 (1964).

16. Social Security Amendments of 1965, Pub. L. No. 89-97, 79 Stat. 286 (codified as amended at 42 U.S.C. §§1395–1395ccc [2010])

17. Social Security Amendments of 1965, Pub. L. No. 89-97, 79 Stat. 286 (codified as amended at 42 U.S.C. §§1396–1396v [2010]).

18. See, e.g., Clean Water Act of 1972, Pub. L. No. 92-500, 86 Stat. 816 (codified as amended in 33 U.S.C. §§1251–1387 [2002]); Nat'l Environmental Policy Act of 1969, Pub. L. No. 91–190, 83 Stat. 852, 42 U.S.C. §§4321–4370; Clean Air Act of 1963, Pub. L. No. 88-206, 77 Stat. 392 (codified as amended in 42 U.S.C. §§7401–7671 [2006]).

19. Endangered Species Act of 1973, Pub. L. No. 93-205, 87 Stat. 884, 16 U.S.C. §§1531–1599 (2006).

20. Employee Retirement Income Security Act of 1974, Pub. L. No. 93-406, 88 Stat. 829, 29 U.S.C. §§1001 et seq. (2000).

21. Occupational Safety and Health Act of 1970, Pub. L. No. 91-596, 84 Stat. 1590 (codified as amended at 29 U.S.C. §§651–78 [2006]).

22. Pub. L. No. 111-148, 124 Stat. 119 (2010).

23. Pub. L. No. 111-203, 124 Stat. 1376 (2010).

24. Labor-Management Relations Act, Pub. L. No. 80-101, 61 Stat. 136 (1947).

25. Administrative Procedure Act, Pub. L. No. 79-404 (1946).

26. See, for example, President Barack Obama, White House Press Conference (Feb. 9, 2009), available at www.whitehouse.gov/the-press-office/press -conference-president (arguing that those "suggest[ing] that FDR was wrong to intervene back in the New Deal" are "fighting battles that I thought were resolved a pretty long time ago").

27. See, for example, "Personal Spending Up, Incomes Stagnant," CBS

News (Mar. 1, 2010), available at www.cbsnews.com/stories/2010/03/01/
business/main6255089.shtml ("For all of 2009, personal incomes actually
fell by 1.7 percent, the weakest showing since the Great Depression year of
1938").

28. See, for example, Motoko Rich, "Few New Jobs as Jobless Rate Rises to
9.8 percent," *New York Times* A1 (Dec. 3, 2010).

29. F. A. Hayek, *The Road to Serfdom: The Definitive Edition* (University of
Chicago Press, 2007) (1944).

30. Milton Friedman, *Capitalism and Freedom* (University of Chicago
Press, 2002) (1962).

1. The Traditional Conception of the Rule of Law

1. See F. A. Hayek, *The Road to Serfdom: The Definitive Edition* (University of Chicago Press, 2007), at 118.

2. See, for example, the World Bank's Policy for Development Policy
Lending (Aug. 2004), available at web.worldbank.org/WBSITE/EXTERNAL
/PROJECTS/EXTPOLICIES/EXTOPMANUAL/0,,contentMDK:20240031
~menuPK:64701633~pagePK:64709096~piPK:64709108~theSitePK
:502184,00.html.

3. See, for example, Guido Pincione, "The Constitution of Non-
Domination," 28 *Social Philosophy and Policy* 261 (2011).

4. For a history of common-carrier regulation, see Richard A. Epstein,
*Principles for a Free Society: Reconciling Individual Liberty with the Common
Good,* ch. 10 (1998).

5. Jeremy Waldron, "Legislation and the Rule of Law," 1 *Legisprudence* 91,
97 (2007) (defending legislation against the charge that it is inconsistent with
the rule of law).

6. See Justinian, *Institutes,* Book I, Title 2, 6 (Oliver Thatcher, ed., 1907).

7. For a discussion of this tension, see Richard A. Epstein, *The Natural
Law Influences on the First Generation of American Constitutional Law: Reflec-
tions of Philip Hamburger's* Law and Judicial Duty (forthcoming).

8. John Locke, *Second Treatise of Government* §25, at 18 (C. B. Macpherson
ed., Hackett 1980) (1690) (emphasis omitted).

9. Robert Lee Hale, "Coercion and Distribution in a Supposedly Non-
Coercive State," 38 *Political Science Quarterly* 470 (1923). See my critique of

Hale's essay in Richard A. Epstein, *Skepticism and Freedom: A Modern Case for Classical Liberalism* 110 (2003).

10. Frank I. Michelman, "Property, Utility, and Fairness: Comments on the Ethical Foundations of 'Just Compensation' Law," 80 *Harvard Law Review* 1165 (1967). Note that even the words "just compensation" are put in scare quotes.

11. On this connection, see Adam Smith, *Lectures on Jurisprudence* (Liberty Fund, 2010).

12. Locke, *supra* note 8, §125, at 66.

13. Id.

14. Id.

15. See Philip Hamburger, *Law and Judicial Duty* 322 (2008).

16. A. V. Dicey, *Introduction to the Study of the Law of the Constitution* 110 (Liberty Classics, 8th ed., 1982) (1915).

17. Hayek, *supra* note 1, at 76, 80.

18. *Thomas Bonham v. Col. of Physicians* (*Dr. Bonham's Case*), 8 Co. Rep. 114 (1610).

19. See id. at 118a.

20. 1 William Blackstone, *Commentaries* *91; *accord* 2 id. at *156–157.

21. Lon L. Fuller, *The Morality of Law* 39 (1964).

22. See, for example, Waldron, *supra* note 5 at 109–112.

23. Henry J. Friendly, "Some Kind of Hearing," 123 *University of Pennsylvania Law Review* 1267, 1279 (1975).

24. See, for example, *Dean Milk v. Madison,* 340 U.S. 349 (1951) (rejecting supposed health justifications for refusing to allow milk pasteurized in Illinois to be sold in Madison, Wisconsin).

25. Herbert Wechsler, "The Challenge of a Model Penal Code," 63 *Harvard Law Review* 1097, 1102 (1952).

26. See Marc I. Miller and Ronald F. Wright, "The Black Box," 94 *Iowa Law Review* 125, 129 (2008).

27. On the limitations, see Chapter 3 in this volume.

28. Miller and Wright, *supra* note 26 at 136.

29. See Richard A. Epstein, *Bargaining with the State* 5 (1993).

30. For discussion, see Richard A. Epstein, "Contingent Commissions in Insurance: A Legal and Economic Analysis," 3 *Competition Policy International* 281 (2007).

31. Bristol-Myers-Squibb Deferred Prosecution Agreement (June 13, 2005),

NOTES TO PAGES 27–37

available at www.usdoj.gov/usao/nj/press/files/pdffiles/deferredpros.pdf

available at www.usdoj.gov/usao/nj/press/files/pdffiles/deferredpros.pdf ("20. BMS shall endow a chair at Seton Hall University School of Law dedicated to the teaching of business ethics and corporate governance").

32. Baron de Montesquieu, *The Spirit of the Laws* 155–164 (Anne M. Cohler, Basia C. Miller, and Harold S. Stone, eds., Cambridge University Press, 1989) (1748).

33. For the classical articulation, see *The Federalist* (Clinton Rossiter, ed., 1961). Elsewhere, the Constitution protects federalism and states' rights. The Tenth Amendment, which some modern cases have sought to make a "truism" (see *United States v. Darby*, 312 U.S. 100, 124 [1941]), provides: "The powers not delegated to the United States by the Constitution, nor prohibited by it to the States, are reserved to the States respectively, or to the people." U.S. Const. Amend. X.

34. John Locke, *Second Treatise of Government*, §144, at 76 (C.B Macpherson ed., 1980) (1690) (emphasis omitted).

2. Reasonableness Standards and the Rule of Law

1. Restatement (Third) of Torts: Liability for Physical Harm §3 (2005). This test is based on the famous decision of Learned Hand in *United States v. Carroll Towing Co.,* 159 F.2d 169 (2d Cir. 1946), which has been championed in Richard A. Posner, "A Theory of Negligence," 1 *Journal of Legal Studies* 29 (1972).

2. For a discussion of the risks, see Richard A. Epstein, *Simple Rules for a Complex World* 92–96 (Harvard University Press, 1995).

3. For the empirical support, see H. Laurence Ross, *Settled Out of Court: The Social Process of Insurance Claims Adjustment* 980–99 (Aldine, 2d ed., 1980).

4. 132 Eng. Rep. 490 (C.P. 1837).

5. For a discussion of the permutations, see Richard A. Epstein, "The Many Faces of Fault in Contract Law: Or How To Do Economics Right, without Really Trying," 107 *Michigan Law Review* 1461 (2009).

6. See Restatement (Second) of Torts, §§479–480.

7. See, for example, *Charbonneau v. MacRury*, 153 A. 457 (N.H. 1931).

8. James Henderson, "Judicial Review of Manufacturer's Conscious Design Choices: The Limits of Adjudication," 73 *Columbia Law Review* 1531 (1973).

9. *Larsen v. Gen. Motors Corp.*, 391 F.2d 495, 500 (8th Cir. 1968).

10. Clarence Morris, "Custom and Negligence," 42 *Columbia Law Review* 1147, 1164–1165 (1942).

11. *Campo v. Scofield*, 95 N.E.2d 802, 804 (N.Y. 1950).

12. A. Mitchell Polinsky and Steven Shavell, "The Uneasy Case for Products Liability," 123 *Harvard Law Review* 1437 (2010); W. Kip Viscusi, *Reforming Products Liability* (1992).

13. *Kline v. 1500 Massachusetts Ave. Apartment Corp.*, 439 F.2d 477 (D.C. Cir. 1970).

14. See, for example, *MacDonald v. Ortho Pharm. Corp.*, 394 Mass. 131, 139 (1985)

15. 129 S. Ct. 1187 (2009). For my comments, see Richard A. Epstein, "What Tort Theory Tells Us about Federal Preemption: The Tragic Saga of *Wyeth v. Levine*," 65 *Annual Survey of American Law* 485 (2010).

3. Where Natural Law and Utilitarianism Converge

1. Justinian, *Institutes*, Book I Title 1, Sec. 3 (Peter Birks and Grant McLeod, eds., Cornell University Press, 1987) ("Iuris praecepta sunt haec: honeste vivere, alterum non laedere, suum cuique tribuere").

2. For a critique of that position, see Robert Pippin, "Natural and Normative," 138 *Daedalus* 3 (Summer 2009).

3. See David Hume, *A Treatise of Human Nature*, Book III (L. A. Selby-Bigge ed., 1949) (1740).

4. N. E. Simmonds, *The Decline of Juridical Reason: Doctrine and Theory in the Legal Order* (Manchester University Press, 1984).

5. For discussion, see Saul Levmore, "Variety and Uniformity in the Treatment of the Good-Faith Purchaser," 16 *Journal of Legal Studies* 43 (1987).

6. Aristotle, *The Nicomachean Ethics*, Book V (William David Ross, trans., Oxford University Press, 1998).

7. See, e.g., *Mitchell v. Reynolds*, 98 Eng. Rep. 347 (1711).

8. Ronald H. Coase, "The Problem of Social Cost," 3 *Journal of Law and Economics* 1 (1960).

9. See Richard A. Epstein, "The Many Faces of Fault in Contract Law: Or How To Do Economics Right, without Really Trying," 107 *Michigan Law Review* 1461 (2009) (describing how ordinary language leads to efficient loss allocation rules).

10. Wikipedia, s.v. "Pecuniary externality," en.wikipedia.org/wiki/Pecuniary_externality.

11. John Stuart Mill, *On Liberty* 72 (Everyman's Ed., 1971) (1859).

4. Where Natural Law and Utilitarianism Diverge

1. For judicial discussion of the various differences, see *Matsushita Elec. Ind. Co. v. Zenith Radio Corp.,* 475 U.S. 574 (1986).

2. National Labor Relations Act of 1935, 74 Pub. L. No. 198, 49 Stat. 449, codified at 29 U.S.C. §159 (1935).

3. See, for example, Agricultural Adjustment Act of 1938, Pub. L. No. 75-430, 52 Stat. 31 (1938).

4. For discussion, see Richard A. Epstein, *Free Markets under Siege: Cartels, Politics, and Social Welfare* (IEA, 2004), (Australia and New Zealand ed., 2004), (Hoover Institution, 2005).

5. For a classic account of this approach, see W. D. Ross, *The Right and the Good* (Phillip Stratton-Lake, ed., Oxford University Press, 2002) (1930).

6. For discussion, see Richard B. Stewart, "The Reformation of American Administrative Law," 88 *Harvard Law Review* 1667 (1975).

7. James M. Landis, *The Administrative Process* (Yale University Press, 1938).

8. For an extensive critique, see Richard A. Epstein, *How Progressives Rewrote the Constitution* (Cato, 2006).

5. Property Rights in the Grand Social Scheme

1. John Locke, *Second Treatise of Government* IX, §123 (C. B. MacPherson, ed., Hackett, 1980) (1690).

2. See Thomas Hobbes, *Leviathan* 84 (Cosimo, 2009) (1651) ("The value of all things contracted for, is measured by the Appetite of the Contractors, and therefore the just value, is that which they be contented to give").

3. For a vivid illustration of the caricature, see Peter S. Menell, "Intellectual Property and the Property Rights Movement," 37 *Regulation* (Fall 2007); for my reply, see Richard A. Epstein, "The Property Rights Movement and Intellectual Property: A Response to Peter Menell," 58 *Regulation* (Winter 2008).

4. See Justinian, *Institutes,* Book II, Title 1 (Peter Birks and Grant McLeod, eds., Cornell University Press, 1987).

5. For a detailed if over-the-top account of the dangers of this fragmentation, see Michael Heller, *The Gridlock Economy: How Too Much Ownership Wrecks Markets, Stops Innovation, and Costs Lives* (Basic Books, 2008), including discussion of the various castles on the Rhine River. The subtitle is misleading because most of the examples of gridlock stem from the use of the government permit power. For my comments on Heller, see Richard A. Epstein, "Heller's Gridlock Economy in Perspective: Why There Is Too Little, Not Too Much, Private Property," 53 *Ariz. L. Rev.* 51 (2011).

6. See *Allnut v. Inglis*, 104 Eng. Rep. 206 (1810) (Ellenborough, C.J.) (announcing the exception to the general rule that was incorporated into American law in *Munn v. Illinois*, 94 U.S. 113 [1876]). For a historical account, see Richard A. Epstein, *Principles for a Free Society: Reconciling Individual Liberty with the Common Good* 282–287 (Basic Books 1998).

7. For a discussion of the various approaches, see *Duquesne Light Co. v. Barasch*, 488 U.S. 299 (1988).

8. See Harold Demsetz, "Why Regulate Utilities?" 11 *Journal of Law and Economics* 1 (1968).

9. See Michael McConnell, "Public Utilities' Private Rights: Paying for Failed Nuclear Power Projects," 2 *Regulation* 35 (1988).

10. See, for example, *Munn v. Illinois*, 94 U.S. 113 (1876).

11. Telecommunications Act of 1996, Pub. L. No. 104-104, 110 Stat. 56, codified at 47 U.S.C. §151 et seq.

12. *Verizon Commc'ns, Inc. v. FCC*, 535 U.S. 467 (2002).

6. The Bundle of Rights

1. See, for example, James Harris, *Property and Justice* 32 (Oxford 1996) ("If deliberate homicide is prohibited, it would never be even a prima facie defence that the murderer was using his own dagger").

2. For one effort, see Richard A. Epstein, "Nuisance Law: Corrective Justice and Its Utilitarian Constraints," 8 *Journal of Legal Studies* 49 (1979).

3. W. A. Hunter, *A Systematic and Historical Exposition of Roman Law* 243 (Sweet and Maxwell, 4th ed., 1903).

4. For the usual formulations, see Restatement (Third) of Torts, Liability for Physical Harm §26 (2005).

5. See *Stone v. Bolton* [1950] 1 K.B. 201 (C.A. 1949), rev'd by *Bolton v. Stone* [1951] A.C. 850, [1951] 1 All E.R. 1078. For a more extended critique of this wa-

tershed decision, see Richard A. Epstein, "A Theory of Strict Liability," 2 *Journal of Legal Studies* 151, 169–189 (1973).

6. See, e.g., *Barker v. Lull Eng'g Co.*, 573 P.2d 443 (Cal. 1978) (allowing design defect action in face of product misuse).

7. *Campo v. Scofield*, 95 N.E. 2d 802, 804 (N.Y. 1950).

8. See John Stuart Mill, *On Liberty* 72 (1859).

9. See *Rideout v. Knox*, 19 N.E. 390, 391 (Mass. 1889).

10. *Corp. of Birmingham v. Allen* [1877] 6 Ch. Div. 284.

11. *Rideout v. Knox*, 19 N.E. at 390. The statute read: "Section 1. Any fence, or other structure in the nature of a fence, unnecessarily exceeding six feet in height, maliciously erected or maintained for the purpose of annoying the owners or occupants of adjoining property, shall be deemed a private nuisance."

12. *Bamford v. Turnley* (1860) 3 B.&S. 62; 122 Eng. Rep. 25 (K.B.). For a more complete account of how this plays out in different physical settings, see Richard A. Epstein, "Property Rights, State of Nature Theory, and Property Protection," 4 *NYU Journal of Law and Liberty* 1 (2008).

13. *Bamford v. Turnley* (1860) 3 B.&S. 62. Note that while Baron Bramwell has the individualist point clearly in mind, his formulation does not distinguish clearly between the Pareto and Kaldor-Hicks account of social welfare.

14. For an illustration of this error, see John Dawson, "Economic Duress," 45 *Michigan Law Review* 253 (1947).

15. See Franklin Roosevelt, "The Economic Bill of Rights," State of the Union Address (Jan. 11, 1944).

16. See, for example, *Post v. Jones*, 60 U.S. 150 (1856).

17. For discussion, see Wayne Brough, "Liability Salvage—by Private Ordering," 19 *Journal of Legal Studies* 95 (1990).

7. Eminent Domain

1. U.S. Const. Amend. V.

2. *Loretto v. TelePromp Ter Manhattan CATV Corp.*, 458 U.S. 419 (1982).

3. *Fisher v. City of Berkeley*, 693 P.2d 261, 294–95 (Cal. 1984) (requiring reasonable economic return on investment).

4. *Helmsley v. Borough of Fort Lee*, 394 A.2d 65 (N.J. 1978) (invalidating ordinance that limited rent increases to 2.5 percent for want of administrative relief in hardship cases).

5. See *Yee v. City of Escondido*, 503 U.S. 519 (1992).

6. See *Roberts v. Tishman Speyer Props.*, L.P., 13 N.Y.3d 270, 918 N.E.2d 900 (2009).

7. See, for example, *Armstrong v. United States*, 364 U.S. 40 (1960).

8. 438 U.S. 104 (1978).

9. See *Penn. Coal Co. v. Mahon*, 260 U.S. 393, 415 (1922).

10. *United States v. Bodcaw Co.*, 440 U.S. 202, 203 (1979) (appraisal fees); *Dohany v. Rogers*, 281 U.S. 362, 368 (1930) (attorney fees).

11. *Kimball Laundry Co. v. United States*, 338 U.S. 1 (1949).

12. See Richard A. Epstein, "Can Anyone Beat the Flat Tax?" 19 *Social Philosophy and Policy* 140 (2002).

13. See, for example, *Head v. Amoskeag Mfg. Co.*, 113 U.S. 9 (1885); *Olmstead v. Camp*, 33 Conn. 532 (1866).

14. See *Strickley v. Highland Boy Gold Mining Co.*, 200 U.S. 527 (1906) (aerial tram over scrub grass); *Clark v. Nash*, 198 U.S. 361 (1905) (irrigation ditch, absolutely necessary to serve land).

15. 348 U.S. 26 (1954).

16. 467 U.S. 229 (1984).

17. 545 U.S. 469 (2005).

18. For details on the response to *Kelo*, see Leonard Gilroy, "*Kelo:* One Year Later," Reason Foundation (June 21, 2006), available at reason.org/news/show/122269.html.

19. For a discussion of the issue, see Richard A. Epstein, "The Wright Stuff," *Regulation* 8 (Spring 2007).

20. Wright Amendment Reform Act of 2006 ("Reform Act"), Pub. L. No. 109–352, 120 Stat. 2011 (2006); see also *Love Terminal Partners, L.P. v. City of Dallas*, 527 F. Supp. 2d 538, 543–47 (N.D. Tex. 2007) (rejecting antitrust challenges to the arrangements protected by the statute).

21. Airline Deregulation Act of 1978, Pub. L. No. 95–504, 92 Stat. 1705, codified at 49 U.S.C. 1551.

22. See, for example, *Kansas v. United States*, 797 F. Supp. 1042, 1051 (D.D.C. 1992) (holding that "Congress imposed the Wright Amendment for rational reasons: to legislatively support a dispute resolution reached by the two cities").

23. Reform Act §5.

24. 173 Fed. Appx. 931 (2d Cir. 2006).

25. For a more comprehensive account, see Richard A. Epstein, "The Permit Power Meets the Constitution," 81 *Iowa Law Review* 407 (1995).

26. See, for example, *Vermont Yankee Nuclear Power Corp. v. Natural Res. Def. Council, Inc.*, 435 U.S. 519 (1975), which sought to prevent lower federal courts from adding endless procedural requirements to licensing proceedings. See also *Natural Res. Def. Council, Inc. v. U.S. Nuclear Regulatory Comm'n*, 547 F.2d 633 (D.C. Cir 1976) (adding additional requirements for "genuine dialogue" between agency officials and objectors). But other grounds still slowed the process. See *Natural Res. Def. Council, Inc. v. U.S. Nuclear Regulatory Comm'n*, 685 F.2d 459 (D.C. Cir. 1982), rev'd *Baltimore Gas & Elec. Co. v. Natural Res. Def. Council, Inc.*, 462 U.S. 87 (1983). Five years of litigation yielded few results. The plant had opened in 1973, so the litigation was solely about the expansion of its rated capacity.

27. See, for example, *Smith v. Town of Mendon*, 822 N.E.2d 1214, 1215 (N.Y. 2004).

28. Doug Kaplan, "Simplify, Don't Subsidize: The Right Way to Support Private Development," Institute for Justice, *Perspectives on Eminent Domain Abuse* 4, *5 (June 2008), available at www.eminentdomainabuse.com/images/publications/perspectives-simplify.pdf.

29. New York City Department of City Planning, The Uniform Land Use Review Procedure (ULURP), see NYC Charter §§197-c and 197-d, available at www.nyc.gov/html/dcp/html/luproc/ulpro.shtml.

30. Id.

31. See *Tahoe-Sierra Pres. Council v. Tahoe Reg'l Planning Agency*, 535 U.S. 302 (2002); *First English Evangelical Church of Glendale v. County of Los Angeles*, 482 U.S. 304 (1986).

32. *Williamson County Reg'l Planning Comm'n v. Hamilton Bank of Johnson City*, 473 U.S. 172 (1985).

33. See, for example, *San Remo Hotel, L.P. v. City & County of San Francisco*, 545 U.S. 323 (2005).

8. Liberty Interests

1. 198 U.S. 45 (1905).

2. N.Y. Stat. §113; see also *Lochner*, 198 U.S. at 46.

3. See *Holden v. Hardy*, 169 U.S. 366 (1898).

4. 45 U.S.C. §54 (2005) (limiting assumption of risk defense in railroad accidents).

5. *Second Employers' Liability Cases,* 223 U.S. 1, 50 (1912).

6. See *Farwell v. Boston & Worcester R.R. Corp.,* 45 Mass. 49 (1842). The rejection of the doctrine came sometimes by statute, and other times by legislation, which was routinely upheld against constitutional attacks based on freedom of contract.

7. *N.Y. Cent. R.R. v. White,* 243 U.S. 188 (1917).

8. See, for example, *Muller v. Oregon,* 208 U.S. 412 (1908).

9. Howard Gillman, *The Constitution Besieged* 62 (Duke, 1993). For a criticism of relying on the class legislation approach and an exhaustive defense of *Lochner,* see David E. Bernstein, *Rehabilitating Lochner: Defending Individual Rights against Progressive Reform* (University of Chicago, 2011).

10. See, for example, *Allgeyer v. Louisiana,* 165 U.S. 578, 589 (1897) (liberty of contract includes not only freedom from physical restraint, but the ability to enter into all contracts to gain a livelihood).

11. See, e.g., *Lamson v. Am. Axe & Tool Co.,* 58 N.E. 585 (Mass. 1900).

12. For discussion, see Richard A. Epstein, "The Historical Origins and Economic Structure of Workers' Compensation," 16 *Georgia Law Review* 775 (1982).

13. See, for example, Richard A. Posner, "A Theory of Negligence," 1 *Journal of Legal Studies* 29 (1972).

14. 9 Q.B.D. 357 (1882).

15. 43 & 44 Vict. Ch. 42.

16. See, for example, 1 T. G. Shearman and A. A. Redfield, *A Treatise on the Law of Negligence,* vi–vii (5th ed., 1898).

17. See, for example, *Coppage v. Kansas,* 236 U.S. 1 (1915); *United States v. Adair,* 208 U.S. 161 (1908).

18. Roscoe Pound, "Liberty of Contract," 18 *Yale Law Journal* 454, 484 (1909).

19. National Labor Relations Act, Pub. L. No. 74-198, 49 Stat. 449, codified at 29 U.S.C. §151 (1935).

20. Fair Labor Standards Act, Pub. L. No. 75-718, 52 Stat. 1060, codified at 29 U.S.C. §201 et seq. (1938).

21. See *National League of Cities v. Usery,* 426 U.S. 833 (1976) (striking down the amendments to the FLSA), overruled by *Garcia v. San Antonio Metropolitan Transit Auth.* 469 U.S. 528 (1985) (sustaining the law).

22. For a glimpse of the issues, see Dep't of Labor, Sheet no. 22, Hours Worked under the Fair Labor Standards Act, www.dol.gov/esa/whd/regs/compliance/whdfs22.pdf. For the full regulations, see 29 U.S.C. §§201–219 (2009).

23. 323 U.S. 134 (1944).

24. Fair Minimum Wage Act of 2007, Pub. L. No. 110-28.

25. See Review and Outlook, "The Lost Wages of Youth," *Wall Street Journal* (Mar. 5, 2010).

26. See National Labor Relations Act, 29 U.S.C. §§151–169.

27. For a complete critique, see Richard A. Epstein, *The Case against the Employee Free Choice Act* (2009).

28. See NLRA, *supra* note 19 at §8(c).

29. See, for example, Alan Blinder, "Our Dickensian Economy," *Wall Street Journal* (Dec. 17, 2010).

9. Positive-Sum Projects

1. See, for example, *Ehrlich v. City of Culver City,* 911 P.2d 429 (Cal. 1996).

2. See *Nollan v. Cal. Coastal Comm'n,* 483 U.S. 825 (1987).

3. For the mechanics, see U.S. Army Corps of Engineers, Compensatory Mitigation Rule: Improving, Restoring, and Protecting the Nation's Wetlands and Streams, www.epa.gov/owow/wetlands/pdf/Mit_rule_QA.pdf.

4. *Nollan,* 483 U.S. 825 (1987).

5. *Dolan v. City of Tigard,* 512 U.S. 374 (1994).

6. See, for example, *Rogers Mach., Inc. v. Washington County,* 45 P.3d 966 (Or. Ct. App. 2002).

7. 444 U.S. 164 (1979).

8. See *Frost v. R.R. Comm'n of State of Cal.,* 271 U.S. 583 (1926). That decision was gutted shortly thereafter in *Stephenson v. Binford,* 287 U.S. 251 (1932).

9. For a historical account of the regulation of jitneys, see Ross D. Eckert and George W. Hilton, "The Jitneys," 15 *Journal of Law and Economics* 296 (1972) (detailing how local street regulation drove jitneys out of business).

10. *In re Opinion of the Justices,* 147 N.E. 681 (Mass. 1925).

11. 515 U.S. 557 (1995).

12. *Mass. Gen. Laws Ann.,* ch. 272, §98 (1992).

13. *Boy Scouts of Am. v. Dale,* 530 U.S. 640 (2000).

14. 130 S. Ct. 2971 (2010). I wrote a brief for the CLS on behalf of the Cato

Institute. For my more extensive views, see Richard A. Epstein, "Church and State at the Crossroads: *Christian Legal Society v. Martinez,*" *Cato Supreme Court Review* 105 (2010).

15. William W. Van Alstyne, "The Demise of the Right-Privilege Distinction in Constitutional Law," 81 *Harvard Law Review* 1439, 1441 (1968).

10. Redistribution Last

1. See John Locke, *Two Treatises of Government,* §§41–42, at 30–32 (David Berman ed., Everyman Paperbacks 1993) (1690).

2. See, J. P. Donlon, "Best/Worst States for Business," chiefexecutive.net/best-worst-states-for-business.

3. See, for example, Meredith Whitney, "State Bailouts? They've Already Begun," *Wall Street Journal* (Nov. 3, 2010).

4. I have discussed these issues in connection with the ill-fated Clinton health plan; see Richard A. Epstein, *Mortal Peril: Our Inalienable Right to Health Care?* (Addison-Wesley, 1997).

5. See Boards of Trustees, Federal Hospital Insurance and Federal Supplementary Medical Insurance Trust Funds, *2010 Annual Report of the Boards of Trustees of the Federal Hospital Insurance and Federal Supplementary Medical Insurance Trust Funds* (2010), with the separate statement by Richard S. Foster, "Statement of Actuarial Opinion," 281, 282 (2010).

6. John D. Shatto and M. Kent Clemens, "Projected Medicare Expenditures under an Illustrative Scenario with Alternative Payment Updates to Medicare Providers," Centers for Medicare and Medicaid Services, May 13, 2011, available at www.cms.gov/ReportsTrustFunds/Downloads/2011TRAlternativeScenario.pdf. The "alternative scenario" discussed in the report involves the restoration of the nominal cuts in reimbursement fees to Medicare providers.

7. See Richard A. Epstein, "Decentralized Responses to Good Fortune and Bad Luck," 9 *Theoretical Inquiries in Law* 309 (Art. 11) (2008), available at www.bepress.com/cgi/viewcontent.cgi?article=1179&context=til.

11. The Rule of Law Diminished

1. For a more systematic account of these issues, which informs the discussion here, see Richard A. Epstein, "Why the Modern Administrative State

Is Inconsistent with the Rule of Law," 3 *NYU Journal of Law and Liberty* 491 (2008).

2. See *Withow v. Larkin,* 421 U.S. 35 (1975).

3. See discussion in Marc I. Miller and Ronald F. Wright, "The Black Box," 94 *Iowa Law Review* 125 (2008).

4. National Labor Relations Act, 29 U.S.C. §§151–169.

5. Under the statutory language in 29 U.S.C. §153(b), it is highly unclear whether three members of the NLRB can delegate their authority to the remaining two just before the third member rotates off. The two-member board was upheld in *Ne. Land Servs. v. NLRB,* 560 F.3d 36 (1st Cir. 2009), petition for cert. filed, No. 09–213 (Aug. 18, 2009), and rejected thereafter in *Laurel Baye Healthcare of Lake Lanier, Inc., v. NLRB,* 564 F.3d 469 (D.C. Cir. 2009).

6. See NLRB, Annual Report, Vol. 14, at 32–33 (1949) (for an early statement).

7. See *Am. Hosp. Ass'n v. NLRB,* 499 U.S. 606 (1991).

8. *Crowell v. Benson,* 285 U.S. 22 (1932).

9. *Martin v. Occupational Safety & Health Review Comm'n,* 499 U.S. 144, 150 (1991).

10. 547 U.S. 715 (2006).

11. 33 U.S.C. §§1311, 1342(a).

12. See 39 Fed. Reg. 12119, codified at 33 C.F.R. §209.120(d)(1) (1974).

13. 33 C.F.R. §328.3(a)(2)–(7) (2004).

14. Id. at 2214 ("The average applicant for an individual permit spends 788 days and $271,596 in completing the process, and the average applicant for a nationwide permit spends 313 days and $28,915—not counting costs of mitigation or design changes"), citing David Sunding and David Zilberman, "The Economics of Environmental Regulation by Licensing: An Assessment of Recent Changes to the Wetland Permitting Process," 42 *Natural Resources Journal* 59, 74–76 (2002).

15. Administrative Procedure Act of 1946, Pub. Law No. 79–404, codified at 5 U.S.C. §706.

16. 467 U.S. 837 (1984).

17. *Natural Res. Def. Council, Inc. v. Gorsuch,* 685 F.2d 718 (D.C. Cir. 1982).

18. See Telecommunications Act of 1996, 47 U.S.C. §§251 and 252 (1996).

19. 5 U.S.C. §706.

20. The two decisions in this matter, rendered some six years apart, were reported at 354 F.2d 608 (2d Cir. 1965) and 453 F.2d 463 (2d Cir. 1971).

21. 401 U.S. 402, (1971).

22. Id. at 416.

23. 15 U.S.C. §1381 et seq.

24. 463 U.S. 29 (1983).

12. Retroactivity

1. For my extended defense of that position, see Richard A. Epstein, "The Disintegration of Intellectual Property? A Classical Liberal Response to a Premature Obituary," 62 *Stanford Law Review* 455 (2010).

2. See U.S. Const., Art. I, §8, cl. 8 ("To promote the Progress of Science and useful Arts, by securing for limited Times to Authors and Inventors the exclusive Right to their respective Writings and Discoveries").

3. See U.S. Const. Art. I, §10, cl. 1 ("No state shall . . . pass any . . . ex post facto Law . . ."). The restriction of the ex post facto prohibition to criminal laws only was settled in *Calder v. Bull,* 3 U.S. 386 (1798).

4. See *Stogner v. California,* 539 U.S. 607, 632–33 (2003), which by a five-to-four vote struck down under the Ex Post Facto Clause of the United States Constitution a state law that removed the protection of the statute of limitations for criminal prosecutions of child abuse.

5. *Sturges v. Crowninshield,* 17 U.S. (4 Wheat.) 122 (1819) (Marshall, C.J.). The Supreme Court refused to extend the Contracts Clause to prospective legislation in *Ogden v. Saunders* 25 U.S. (12 Wheat.) 213 (1827) (Marshall, C.J., dissenting). I have defended a modified version of the Marshall and Story position; see Richard A. Epstein, "Toward a Revitalization of the Contract Clause," 51 *University of Chicago Law Review* 703, 729–747 (1984).

6. See Cal. Civ. Pro. §340.1, which allowed a one-year window in which a person could bring a sexual abuse case that had been barred by the statute of limitation. The statute was held constitutional with respect to claims that had not been reduced to final judgment, but unconstitutional with respect to those which had been so litigated. See *Perez v. Richard Roe 1,* 52 Cal. Rptr. 3d 762 (Cal. App. 2006).

7. See *City of Boston v. Keene Corp.,* 547 N.E.2d 328 (Mass. 1989) (allowing a four-year revival for asbestos-removal claims that the local government brought against asbestos manufacturers).

8. 86 Stat. 150, 30 U.S.C. §901 et seq. (1970 ed. and Supp. IV).

9. *R.R. Ret. Bd. v. Alton R.R. Co.,* 295 U.S. 330 (1935).

10. 428 U.S. 1 (1976).

11. Id. at 16.

12. Id. at 18.

13. Id. at 15.

14. 524 U.S. 498 (1998).

15. See, for example, *Swisher Int'l, Inc. v. Schafer*, 550 F.3d 1046, 1052–55 (2008) (distinguishing *Eastern Enterprises*).

16. 290 U.S. 398 (1934).

17. *Connolly v. Pension Benefit Guar. Corp.*, 475 U.S. 211 (1986); *Pension Benefit Guar. Corp. v. R.A. Gray & Co.*, 467 U.S. 717 (1984).

18. *Connolly*, 475 U.S. at 227.

13. Modern Applications

1. Dodd-Frank Wall Street Reform and Consumer Protection Act, Pub. L. No. 111–203, 124 Stat. 1376 (2010).

2. Patient Protection and Affordable Care Act (ACA), Pub. L. No. 111–148, 124 Stat. 119 (2010).

3. For an excellent overview of the basic statutory provisions, see C. Boyden Gray, "The Dodd-Frank Wall Street Reform and Consumer Protection Act of 2010: Is It Constitutional?" 11 *Engage: The Journal of the Federalist Society's Practice Groups*, 3 (2010).

4. Dodd-Frank, at §111.

5. For the ambiguities in this concept, see Kenneth E. Scott, George P. Shultz, and John Taylor, *Ending Government Bailouts as We Know Them* (Hoover Institution 2010).

6. Dodd-Frank, at §120(a).

7. Id. at §102 (4).

8. Id. at §113(a)(1).

9. *Panama Refining v. Ryan*, 293 U.S. 388 (1935).

10. *A.L.A. Schechter Poultry Corp. v. United States*, 295 U.S. 495 (1935).

11. *Yakus v. United States*, 321 U.S. 414 (1944).

12. Dodd-Frank, at §113 (f).

13. Id. at §113 (h).

14. See *Motor Vehicle Manufacturers' Association v. State Farm Mutual Automobile Insurance Co.* 463 U.S. 29 (1983).

15. Pub. L. No. 111–148, 124 Stat. 119 (2010).

16. For a defense of this view, see Richard A. Epstein and David A. Hyman, "Controlling the Cost of Medical Care: A Dose of Deregulation," available online at http://papers.ssrn.com/sol3/papers.cfm?abstract_id=1158547.

17. U.S. Census Bureau, *Income, Poverty, and Health Insurance Coverage in the United States: 2009*, at *22, available at www.census.gov/prod/2010pubs/p60–238.pdf.

18. I.R.C. §5000A (2010). There are similar, and equally complex, mandates for employers who have more than fifty employees, at least one of whom receives some federal support. These have not generated anything like the protest to the individual mandates. See ACA at §1513 for the gory details.

19. Kaiser Health Tracking Poll, Questions 14–16, Kaiser Family Foundation (Aug. 2010), available at www.kff.org/kaiserpolls/upload/8093-T.pdf (indicating that of fifteen elements of the ACA, the requirement "that nearly all Americans . . . have health insurance or pay a fine" is viewed least favorably by a substantial margin).

20. U.S. Const. art. I, §8, cl. 3.

21. See *Wickard v. Filburn,* 317 U.S. 111 (1942), which presented that fact pattern. The back-story to the case was that wheat growers and cattle farmers vertically integrated to undermine the cartel that the Roosevelt administration sought to set up under the Agricultural Adjustment Acts.

22. See *Virginia v. Sebelius,* 702 F. Supp. 2d 598 (2010).

23. Mancur Olson, *The Logic of Collective Action: Public Goods and the Theory of Groups* (1965).

24. Under the ACA and its amendments, health insurance will be mandatory, barring some exceptions, for all citizens by 2014. The penalty, to be phased in gradually, will reach a peak of the greater of $695 for an individual, $2,085 for a family, or 2.5 percent of household income. See Health Care and Education Reconciliation Act of 2010, Pub L. No. 111–152, 124 Stat. 1029, §1002.

25. See Alain Enthoven, *Theory and Practice of Managed Competition in Health Care* 5 (1988) (italics in original). For my criticism of the social-insurance model, see Richard A. Epstein, *Mortal Peril: Our Inalienable Right to Health Care?* 43–59 (1997).

26. See ACA at §1101 (concerning immediate access to insurance for uninsured individuals with preexisting conditions); and ACA §2704 (Prohibition of Preexisting Condition Exclusions or Other Discrimination Based on Health Care Status).

27. See ACA at §2702 (guaranteed availability of coverage).

28. Id. at §2701 (a)(1)(iii). The act also requires nonsmokers to subsidize smokers; id. at §2701 (a)(1)(iv).

29. Id. at §1311(a).

30. Id. at §1311(d).

31. Id. at §1311(c).

32. Id. at §2718(b). For the administration regulations, see 75 Fed. Reg., 230 (Dec. 1, 2010) (to be codified at 45 C.F.R. 158), available at edocket.access. gpo.gov/2010/pdf/2010–29596.pdf.

33. On which, see *Fed. Power Comm'n v. Hope Natural Gas,* 320 U.S. 591 (1944) and *Duquesne Light Co. v. Barasch,* 488 U.S. 299 (1989).

34. For discussion, see David R. Henderson, *Mini-Med Plans,* Brief Analysis No. 727, National Center for Policy Analysis (Oct. 21, 2010), available at www.ncpa.org/pdfs/ba727.pdf.

35. Janet Adamy, "McDonald's May Drop Health Plan," *Wall Street Journal* (Sept. 30, 2010).

36. Dept. of Health and Human Servs., Office of Consumer Information and Insurance Oversight Guidance (Dec. 10, 2010), available at www.health-care.gov/center/regulations/guidance_limited_benefit_2nd_supp_bulle-tin_120910.pdf.

Index of Cases

General Index

Arbitrary and capricious decisions, 7, 159–163, 178

Arbitrary power, 10, 13–14, 17, 61, 191

Aristotle, 49–50

Army Corps of Engineers, 155–156

Articulation of rules, 7, 11, 14–15, 19–21, 29, 43–44, 95, 159, 191

Association, freedom of, 137–138

Automobile industry, 128–129, 162–163, 178

Autonomy, 45, 47, 61, 182

Bad faith, 34

Bailouts, 145, 173

Banking industry, 173

Bank of America, 173

Bankruptcy, 169, 174, 178

Bargaining units, 152–153

Bias, 9, 18–20, 147, 150–153, 166, 173, 175

Bible, 13

Black Lung Benefits Act, 167

Blackstone, William, 19

Bologna, Dominick, 112

Bonham, Thomas, 18

Boundary lines, 80, 85–86, 88

Bramwell, Baron (George Wilshere), 87, 203n13

"Brandeis" briefs, 123

Brennan, William, 104

Bristol-Myers-Squibb, 27

Bundle of rights, 8, 58, 74, 77–96, 103, 144

California, 116, 136, 144, 210n6

Capital markets, 2–3, 5, 9

Cartels, 2, 55–57, 121, 212n21

Carter, Jimmy, 157, 162

Cash compensation, 58–60, 107, 118

Catholics, 137

Causation, 81–82

Centralized state planning, 11

Change, 12

Charlotte, N.C., 24

Chase Bank, 173

Checks and balances, 28

Child abuse, 165, 210nn4,6

Christian Legal Society, 138–139

Christie, Christopher, 27

Citibank, 173

Civil Code (Germany), 76

Civil law, 80

Civil proceedings/sanctions, 2–3, 6, 20–22, 24–25, 94, 159–160, 166

Civil Rights Act, 3

Civil War, 125

Clans, 15–16

Clarity, 7, 14–15, 19–21, 95, 159, 191

Class actions, 26–27, 49, 100

Classifications of persons/groups, 22–23, 123, 126–127, 144, 151

Clayton Antitrust Act, 2

Clean Air Act, 157

Clean Water Act, 155

Coal Industry Retiree Health Benefit Act, 169

Coase, Ronald, 51, 92

Coercion, 14, 18, 22, 27, 46–48, 51–52, 54, 58, 73, 93, 97–98, 106–107, 128–132, 153–154, 182

Coke, Edward, 18–19

Collective bargaining, 2, 56, 125–126, 128

Commerce Clause, 181

Commodities Futures Trading Commission, 175

Common carriers, 11, 121, 136, 138

Common employment, 122

Common law, 19, 37, 50, 73, 135, 144, 151,